Texting, Suicide, and the Law

AF694822

In 2014, Conrad Roy committed suicide following encouragement from his long-distance girlfriend, Michelle Carter, in what has become known as the Texting Suicide case. The case has attracted much attention, largely focusing on the First Amendment free speech issue. This book takes the view that the issue is intertwined with several others, some of which have received less attention but help explain why the case is so captivating and important, issues concerning privacy, accountability, coercion, punishment, and assisted suicide. The focus here is on how all of these issues are interconnected. By breaking the issue down into its complex layers, the work aids reasoned judgment, ensuring we aren't guided solely by our gut reactions. The book is laid out as a case against punishing Ms. Carter, but it is less important that we agree with that conclusion than that we reach our conclusions not just through our instincts and intuitions but by thinking about these fundamental issues. The work will be of interest to scholars in law, political theory, and philosophy as an example of how theory can be applied to particular controversies. It will also appeal to readers interested in freedom of speech and the First Amendment, criminal justice and theories of punishment, suicide laws, and privacy.

Mark Tunick is Professor of Political Science and Associate Dean at the Wilkes Honors College of Florida Atlantic University, USA, where he teaches political theory and constitutional law.

Texting, Suicide, and The Law

The case against punishing Michelle Carter

Mark Tunick

Routledge
Taylor & Francis Group
LONDON AND NEW YORK

First published 2019 by Routledge

2 Park Square, Milton Park, Abingdon, Oxfordshire OX14 4RN
52 Vanderbilt Avenue, New York, NY 10017

Routledge is an imprint of the Taylor & Francis Group, an informa business

First issued in paperback 2020

Copyright © 2019 Mark Tunick

The right of Mark Tunick to be identified as author of this work has been asserted by him in accordance with sections 77 and 78 of the Copyright, Designs and Patents Act 1988.

All rights reserved. No part of this book may be reprinted or reproduced or utilised in any form or by any electronic, mechanical, or other means, now known or hereafter invented, including photocopying and recording, or in any information storage or retrieval system, without permission in writing from the publishers.

Notice:
Product or corporate names may be trademarks or registered trademarks, and are used only for identification and explanation without intent to infringe.

British Library Cataloguing-in-Publication Data
A catalogue record for this book is available from the British Library

Library of Congress Cataloging-in-Publication Data
A catalog record for this book has been requested

ISBN: 978-0-367-19740-7 (hbk)
ISBN: 978-0-367-54642-7 (pbk)

Typeset in Times New Roman
by Apex CoVantage, LLC

Contents

Preface vii

1 Introduction 1

The issue: should Michelle Carter be punished? 1
Background 5
Four underlying issues 16
Privacy 16
Causation and coercion 17
Punishment 17
Suicide laws 17

2 Privacy 19

The privacy issue 19
The prima facie case for privacy 22
The value of privacy 23
Michelle's and Conrad's interest in privacy is legitimate 27
Reasonable expectations of privacy 28
Reasonable expectations of privacy in texts 29
Balancing privacy against competing interests 35
The need to balance 35
The interest in moral punishment 37
The interest in legal punishment 39

3 Causation and coercion 40

The issue 40
Framing the legal question 41
Ms. Carter did not commit manslaughter by omission 42
Ms. Carter did not commit manslaughter by commission 44

Was her conduct reckless? *44*
Causation *45*
But for cause *45*
Proximate cause *47*
The voluntary intervention principle *54*
Encouraging and inciting vs. advising *55*
Coercion *62*
Conclusion: can words kill? *67*

4 Punishment 70
Overview *70*
Retributive purposes of punishment *73*
Kant and Hegel *73*
Mabbott *76*
Legal moralism *77*
The case against legal moralism *79*
Utilitarian purposes of punishment *84*
Conclusion *88*

5 Suicide laws 90
Overview *90*
The utilitarian argument: is suicide always a bad consequence? *92*
Did Ms. Carter act badly in encouraging suicide? *96*
The theistic and other arguments that suicide is wrong *97*
The liberal pluralist argument against suicide laws *99*
An example: oyako shinju *101*
The First Amendment Establishment Clause objection to suicide laws *102*
Encouraging, advising, assisting *105*

6 Conclusion 107
Haidt's argument: reason vs. intuition *109*
Privacy *110*

Index 112

Preface

This book applies political, moral, and legal theories to a hot-button issue that has made the news internationally: whether a teenage girl, Michelle Carter, should be punished for encouraging her friend Conrad Roy to take his own life. The case raises important issues concerning the rights to privacy and free speech. We may disagree about whether suicide is necessarily wrong, depending on our religious and moral convictions, and so the case also forces us to think about a fundamental question of political theory: should the state take sides and favor some religious or philosophical views over others?

Routledge's Focus series allows authors to provide timely responses to contemporary issues concisely and in a format accessible to students and practitioners. There is an inherent danger in introducing theories that are rigorously analyzed and debated by specialized scholars to a much wider audience. It becomes difficult to attend to the details of the debates among philosophers and theorists while holding the attention of this broader audience. I believe that theory has value insofar as it can guide us in our lives, and so to me the goal of bringing theory to bear on a practical controversy is worth some compromises. While I make demands on the reader by presenting some challenging arguments about privacy, causation, punishment, and the proper use of state powers, I do not attempt to address all their nuances and instead leave readers interested in exploring their complexities to consult additional literature. The concise format requires some other compromises as well. I cannot discuss all the philosophical and legal issues the Carter case raises, and so I have made choices. For example, I do not examine how gendered power dynamics may have played out in this case. And while I discuss the implications to our right to speak freely if the state punishes Ms. Carter for texting and speaking words of encouragement, I do not provide a comprehensive review of First Amendment case law.

I take up a very controversial issue. When I presented the case in a lecture to 150 undergraduates and took an initial poll as to whether Michelle should or should not be punished, the response was a virtual tie. As I will note repeatedly throughout the book, it is less important to me that we agree with my conclusion that she should not be legally punished than that we think through the underlying issues of political, moral, and legal theory the case raises and not judge Ms. Carter solely based on immediate, instinctive reactions. Theory matters. On February 11, 2019, Ms. Carter began a prison sentence even as her attorneys planned to file an appeal to the U.S. Supreme Court. The outcome of this last-ditch appeal may be finally decided even as this book is in press, but the underlying issues will be with us for generations.

I thank the editors of Routledge for making the Focus platform available and encouraging me to pursue this project, and I thank its anonymous reviewers, as well as the many colleagues and students who heard me out on the Carter case and offered objections that led me to sharpen my own position, especially Ashley Kennedy and Andrew Faris.

1 Introduction

The issue: should Michelle Carter be punished?

Eighteen-year-old Conrad Roy had suicidal thoughts for some time. His long-distance girlfriend, Michelle Carter, had exchanged texts with him for close to two years, and in her texts up through June of 2014 she tried to lift his spirits and encouraged him to seek help. But Conrad remained profoundly unhappy, and she appears to have become frustrated that nothing she said helped to bring him out of his depression. In late June or early July 2014, Ms. Carter's texts took a sharp turn. She began to encourage Conrad to end his life, even texting him advice on the most effective suicide methods. She complained that he kept putting it off and told him he just had to go through with it. It appears that on July 12, after Conrad turned on a water pump he rigged to release carbon monoxide gas into his truck, and sat inside, he got scared, stepped out, and spoke on the phone with Michelle. She told him to get back in the truck. Sometime after that conversation, Conrad died of carbon monoxide poisoning. After police learned that Michelle encouraged Conrad to kill himself, they arrested her. Prosecutors tried her for involuntary manslaughter, claiming her words caused Conrad's death, and she was found guilty. My attention in this book is focused on the question, should Michelle Carter be punished?

In asking that question I really have three more specific questions in mind. First, does Ms. Carter deserve our criticism and scorn? In other words, should she receive moral punishment and a bad reputation for having acted badly?

Not all individuals who deserve to be morally reproached should be punished by the state. Whereas moral punishment is delivered by individuals on those who act badly, as defined by whoever is doing the judging, and without any procedures for the accused to defend themselves, or for ensuring the punishment is fair and just, legal punishment is meted out by the state only upon those accused of violating a law, after a determination of guilt that provides for due process and the opportunity for a trial. The second question we might mean in asking whether Ms. Carter should be punished, then, is: was she guilty of breaking a law and therefore deserving of legal punishment?

Even if a person is convicted for violating a law, we might think the state should not have enacted that law and that the conduct the law prohibits should not be a punishable offense; and so yet another question we might mean in asking whether Ms. Carter should be punished is whether there ought to be a law against what she did. I will address each of these questions. In asking whether Ms. Carter should be punished one might also mean, ought we to punish those who violate the law as opposed to responding in some other way? But even though there are some interesting criticisms of the very practice of legal punishment, I will assume that we should punish those who violate the law.

The Carter case has generated extraordinary public interest and garnered international attention, sparking divisive emotional responses ranging from anger at Ms. Carter to outrage at her conviction. When Ms. Carter was released pending her appeal, family members of Mr. Roy were furious. What kind of person would tell their close friend to get into a truck filling with poisonous gas? On the other hand, can words really kill? Even if we agree that Ms. Carter acted badly – though her texts indicate that she thought Conrad would be happier if he ended his life – is that sufficient reason to use the force of law to punish her? Punishing Ms. Carter would express the rage many people feel toward her for her apparent cruelty, and it may deter others from encouraging suicide. Yet if we punish people for what they say to their loved ones in private, won't that undermine our right to speak freely without fear of reprisal, and hinder our ability to have meaningful personal relationships?

Much of the attention the case has drawn focuses on the First Amendment issue of whether we should punish someone for their words. The First Amendment prohibits government from "abridging the freedom of speech," and putting someone in prison because she spoke or texted what was on her mind would seem to constitute such an abridgement; it would likely limit the speech of other people as well who would fear receiving similar treatment. The First Amendment protects speech, but there are recognized exceptions. For example, malicious libel or true threats, while speech, can be prohibited. Another recognized category of speech that can subject the speaker to punishment is speech integral to criminal conduct. In *Giboney v. Empire Storage and Ice Company*, a union of ice peddlers who purchased ice from Empire and other suppliers sought to pressure the suppliers to agree to sell only to union peddlers. Such an agreement would violate a state law prohibiting restraints of trade. Empire refused, and the union then promptly picketed the company, causing it to lose 85% of its business. While we might think that the First Amendment gives union members the right to try to persuade businesses to change their behavior, the U.S. Supreme Court determined that in this case the union was coercing Empire to commit a crime. The Court unanimously held that the union had no First Amendment right to engage in speech integral to criminal conduct: "It rarely has been suggested that the constitutional freedom for speech and press extends its immunity to speech or writing used as an integral part of conduct in violation of a valid criminal statute."[1] Whether Michelle's speech does or does not deserve First Amendment protection – an issue I will not focus on – may hinge on the issue I do focus on: whether Ms. Carter's speech was integral to criminal conduct and deserving of punishment.

Many of the issues I will focus on have received less attention than the First Amendment issue, but help explain why the case is so captivating and important, issues concerning privacy, causation, coercion, punishment, and suicide laws: should the intimate exchanges between Michelle and Conrad have remained private, as they were intended to be? While privacy is valuable, it should not be a shield for wrongful conduct, but in encouraging Conrad to take his own life did Ms. Carter commit a crime? Did her words cause Conrad's death, or was Conrad ultimately responsible by voluntarily getting back into his truck and poisoning himself? If Michelle believed that suicide would relieve Conrad of unbearable suffering, did she even act badly? Of course many people regard suicide as wrong, and judge Michelle harshly for encouraging this wrong: but should the fact that the majority judges an individual's actions to be immoral or sinful mean that the individual should be legally punished? The case serves as a touchstone for addressing fundamental issues of political, moral, and legal theory with implications broader than whether Ms. Carter goes to prison.

When we first learn about the Carter case we may have an intuitive reaction. One New England resident compared Ms. Carter to Saddam Hussein: "I'm not a religious guy, but if there's evil, that was evil."[2] Others may feel that Michelle meant well, having seen Conrad suffer so much. Intuitive reactions are powerful. They can be helpful guides in making decisions; but they also can hinder our ability to make reasoned judgments.

Jonathan Haidt, a social psychologist, argues that we adopt our political or moral stances largely based on our intuition. By evolutionary design, on his view, we intrinsically judge others instinctually and only later do we offer post-hoc rationalizations. He uses the metaphor of the elephant and

1 336 US 490, 498 (1949). For further discussion see Eugene Volokh, "The Speech Integral to Criminal Conduct," *Cornell Law Review* 101(4):981–1052 (2016).

2 Quoted in Jesse Baron, "The Girl from Plainville," *Esquire* (October 2017), p. 105.

the rider. The elephant is moved by emotion, intuition, and "taste receptors," while the rider, who emerged later in our evolutionary history, has higher cognitive functions including language and reason. Rather than the rider using these higher cognitive abilities to steer the elephant, Haidt argues, the rider serves the elephant. We reach decisions by relying on our pre-reflective intuitions – our elephant's gut feelings – and our rider merely rationalizes these decisions after the fact. Haidt suggests that many conservatives have an instinctive affinity for what he calls an ethic of divinity – they believe that we must not do what degrades or dishonors God. Haidt might predict that they will judge Ms. Carter harshly for failing to respect the sanctity of life. Haidt suggests that some liberals, in contrast, have a taste or uncritical affinity for autonomy and individual rights; he might predict that they will instinctively defend Ms. Carter, so long as she did not coerce Conrad, and then defend this reaction with rationalizations such as that she is entitled to speak her mind and Conrad has the right to take his own life if he chooses. Haidt's point is that we come to issues such as this guided by emotion and intuition rather than reason.[3]

By breaking down the issue of whether Ms. Carter should be punished into its complex layers, my hope is to aid in reasoned judgments, so we aren't guided solely by our immediate intuitions. I will present the case against punishing Ms. Carter. But it is less important to me that we agree with that conclusion than that we reach our conclusions not just based on our instincts and intuitions but by thinking about these fundamental issues.

Both our intuitive reactions and our reasoned judgments will depend on the facts of the case. Whether we think Ms. Carter should be punished may depend on her motivations, on whether she would expect Conrad to heed her words, on how she intended them, and on our assessment of Conrad's mental state and ability to make decisions for himself. It would surely depend on whether Conrad immediately got into his truck after Michelle told him to and died right then, or whether he shut off the water pump as he got back in his truck, drove around to think, and then killed himself. As with any reconstruction of a past event with few witnesses, the facts may be uncertain. Most of the news reports about the case have relied on some of the more sensational texts in which Ms. Carter urges Conrad to kill himself, but ignore the hundreds of earlier texts in which she begged him to get help and tried to make him feel more positive about himself. I will draw on all the texts that are publicly available, to minimize the risk that the judgments we form about the case rest on inaccurate snippets.[4]

3 Jonathan Haidt, *The Righteous Mind* (New York: Vintage Books, 2012), pp. xix–xx, 54, 62–3, chs. 5–6.

4 The complete set of texts entered into the court record were made available online by several news agencies, and I draw from the texts made available at https://perma.cc/V62U-BURX.

Background

When she was 15, Michelle Carter met 16-year-old Conrad Roy in Naples, Florida, as she was visiting her grandparents and Conrad was visiting his great-aunt a few doors down.[5] Coincidentally they both lived in Massachusetts: Conrad in Mattapoisett, and Michelle in Plainville, about 50 miles away. They began a long-distance relationship mainly consisting of texting each other. It was probably a stressful relationship for Michelle, because Conrad had been suicidal and Michelle herself was struggling with an eating disorder.

Conrad had texted Michelle as early as October of 2012 that he tried to kill himself; and his suicidal thoughts persisted. In one of his texts to Michelle he says "I kinda wish I didn't exist" (6/20/14, 2pm); and in another, that "every time I get depressed my mind takes over and I eventually want to kill myself" (6/21/14, 11:48am). In late June of 2014 they had the following exchanges:

6/25/14, 12:08pm:
MICHELLE: When are we hanging out
CONRAD: Idk yet
MICHELLE: Soon tho right?
CONRAD: Yeah if nothing bad happens to me
MICHELLE: What do you mean?
CONRAD: the past 3 days that's all I can think about and it's in my head now
MICHELLE: Thinking about what? Killing yourself?
CONRAD: Yes

6/29/14, 6:58pm:
CONRAD: you're not suicidal tho are you
MICHELLE: No I'm not. I kinda used to be but I'm not anymore don't worry
CONRAD: I am . . . I just really don't feel like living. I have nothing to live for
MICHELLE: I know you say you're suicidal and say you don't feel like living and stuff but you're never actually gonna do it.
CONRAD: I've tried recently. . .
MICHELLE: What do you mean you've tried? How have you tried? And you're not successful because you know you don't really wanna die
CONRAD: I tried to water intoxication. but you don't know how serious I am, I want to really bad. the past week I've been researching. and if I'm gonna do it it has to be done its nothing you did, like you tried to

5 Baron, "The Girl from Plainville," p. 130.

help. but you don't get where I'm coming from. I've been in mental hospitals and they fuckin suck there's something wrong with my head seriously. . .

7:40pm:

CONRAD: . . . I tried overdosing you know that . . . I took enough to kill me but they got me to the hospital in enough time to treat me, I was 2 hours away from dying . . . there's nothing anyone can do for me that's gonna make me wanna live. It's very bad to hear, but I want to let you know that. Truthfully. I haven't been happy with myself ever. I have split personalities and I don't know who I am . . . I WANT TO DIE.

7/1/14, 11:27pm:

CONRAD: I thought about jumping off the boat.

MICHELLE: That wouldn't do anything.

CONRAD: I know I'm stupid.

MICHELLE: You're not stupid. You're lonely, but you're not alone.

Michelle repeatedly tried to dissuade Conrad from trying to kill himself, up through the end of June 2014. On June 1, she texts Conrad: "Have you thought about getting professional help?" She suggests they go together to McLean hospital in Belmont, where she was planning to receive treatment for her eating disorder: "Let's get better and fight this together . . . Please come . . . I want you to be happy." She then makes him promise that he won't become suicidal again.

Numerous other texts demonstrate that up until the end of June or early July, Michelle tried to help Conrad cope with his depression in positive ways and discouraged him from ending his life:

6/20/14, 1:01pm:

MICHELLE: You need to know that you are loved and wanted every second of every day not just by me, but by so many people

6/22/14, 12:56pm:

MICHELLE: You're in a dark tunnel but it's not gonna last forever. You'll find the light someday and I'm gonna be here to help you find it. You didn't fuck up your life and you aren't a fuck up. You're just lost. But you're gonna be found again I'll never stop looking. You're gonna get thru this okay? I believe in you so much, I love you

CONRAD: I don't believe in myself that's the problem

6/23/14, 12:58pm:

CONRAD: I'm thinking about harming myself to be completely honest.

MICHELLE: Have you ever done it before? Don't because once u start its like impossible to stop and u get scars. I have scars . . . What is harming yourself gonna do!? Nothing! It will just make it worse! . . . I love you

6/25/14, 1:09pm:

MICHELLE: One day at a time, do something that makes you happy. Look at an old photograph and try to remember that moment. Listen to music that shows you're not alone, that people have been thru hard times too. Look at yourself in the mirror everyday and tell yourself you're worth it, that you will get better and overcome this . . . Will you try that?

CONRAD: Yes I'll try it.

6/26/14, 6:05pm:

MICHELLE: Conrad you're not gonna do anything right?

CONRAD: I don't want to talk to you because I feel like I'm getting you upset and bringing you down. . .

MICHELLE: No you aren't! . . . I need you to talk to me . . . right now I need to know that you're okay and aren't gonna do anything so please tell me that.

CONRAD: No I'm not. I want to, but I know I'm not.

7:38pm:

CONRAD: We should be like Romeo and Juliet at the end.

MICHELLE: Haha I'd love to be your Juliet

CONRAD: but do you know what happens at the end

MICHELLE: OH YEAH FUCK NO! WE ARE NOT DYING

CONRAD: lol

Up to this point in late June, Michelle dissuades Conrad from committing suicide, suggests how he might cope, and reminds him that he is loved. But one senses that she is getting frustrated, as nothing seems to be helping. Her frustration is apparent in this exchange in the early afternoon of June 29:

6/29/14, 1:38pm:

CONRAD: . . . nothing makes me happy anymore . . . so I'm stuck in this deep hole

MICHELLE: I'm trying my best to dig you out

CONRAD: I don't wanna be dug out. . .

MICHELLE: I don't know what you want me to do anymore

CONRAD: Nothing you've done plenty. . .
MICHELLE: Well I'm not just gonna leave you

That evening, perhaps because she is so frustrated, she challenges Conrad. He keeps talking about wanting to kill himself, and he made some half-hearted attempts in the past, and she calls his bluff: if he really wanted to kill himself, there are methods he could try that would get the job done, and she now offers advice about some of them. Her intention in the following exchanges is open to interpretation. As we will see, she later suggests that her goal ultimately was not for Conrad to succeed in killing himself, but it was either to push him to the point where he admits he doesn't really want to kill himself, or to have him make another attempt that will be serious enough that he will be hospitalized and receive treatment, but not serious enough that he succeeds.

6/29/14, 8pm:
CONRAD: I WANT TO DIE
MICHELLE: I know you want to! But I just don't get why you're still holding on if you want to so badly. I know you want to and you research it and everything but are you actually really gonna do it?
CONRAD: Yah. If I can find a way to 100% work
MICHELLE: There is though, you're just afraid of doing it . . . What about hanging yourself or stabbing yourself.
CONRAD: I have nowhere to do that
MICHELLE: Yeah you do
CONRAD: well the kid I'm talking to tried it and to didn't work for him [referring to someone from Britain he had been in touch with about ways to commit suicide; see text of 6/30/14, 9:51am]
MICHELLE: Well if you wanted it bad enough then you'd at least try it right? What about over dosing on sleeping pills? Or suffocating with a plastic bag? . . . Sleeping pills would work
CONRAD: really?
MICHELLE: You say you wanna die so bad Conrad, but you aren't willing to try any ways to die. . .
CONRAD: . . . I just don't wanna fail again. That's what I'm scared of . . . I don't wanna be in the mental hospital again. That's why.

9:02pm:
MICHELLE: . . . But the mental hospital would help you. I know you don't think it would but I'm telling you, if you give them a chance they can save your life. *Part of me wants you to try something and fail just so you can go get help . . .* (emphasis added)

Here Michelle begins to offer advice to Conrad about how he could kill himself, but she still is expressing concern for him, and a desire that he get better. Minutes after this last exchange she seeks assurance that he will not try to hurt himself that night:

9:19pm:
MICHELLE: Are you gonna be okay tonight?
CONRAD: Yes I won't do anything

As of July 2, Michelle still tried to dissuade Conrad from ending his life: "There's no way I can change your mind about this?" (7/2, 6:36pm).

Two days later, though, she seems to become impatient and aggressive with him after he again backed down from an attempt on his life:

7/4/14, 10:22am:
CONRAD: don't feel like an idiot it's gonna happen
MICHELLE: Tonight?
CONRAD: eventually
MICHELLE: Cute ☺ haha I love you. SEE THAT'S WHAT I MEAN. YOU KEEP PUSHING IT OFF! You just said you were gonna do it tonight and now you're saying eventually. . .

The sentence in CAPS has been quoted in the press in isolation, without the previous emoticon and comment.[6] Taken by itself it looks like an aggressive effort to pressure Conrad. But it can also be read, in the context of the entire text, as Michelle trying to prove her point that Conrad doesn't really want to die. There is a similar text five days later:

7/9/14, 4:59pm:
MICHELLE: But I bet you're gonna be like 'oh, it didn't work because I didn't tape the tube right or something like that' . . . I bet you're gonna say an excuse like that

Michelle, here, may be earnestly pressuring Conrad to go through with the attempt; or she may just be annoyed at him for continuing to talk about suicide when it seems to her that he does not really mean to kill himself. Her text of June 29 suggests that she might want to encourage him to try something that would require him to be hospitalized, so he could receive therapy.

6 For example: www.cnn.com/2017/06/08/us/text-message-suicide-michelle-carter-conrad-roy/index.html, accessed 11/29/2018.

After Conrad died, Michelle came up with still another explanation of why she encouraged suicide: she was using reverse psychology. The following texts to Michelle's friend Samantha Boardman were sent just over a week after Conrad's death:

7/21, 10:29pm:

MICHELLE: But Sam I'm kinda freaking out about something

SAM: what's wrong?

MICHELLE: I just got off the phone with Conrads mom about 20 mins ago and she told me that detectives had to come and go thru his things and stuff, Its something they have to do with suicides and homicides. And she said they have to go thru his phone and see if anyone encouraged him do it on texts and stuff . . . Sam they read my messages with him, I'm done. His family will hate me and I could go to jail

SAM: Don't worry . . . They will see how he was gonna do it despite what others said . . . unless it was like really bad like bullying. Which it was the opposite of

MICHELLE: Yeah that's what I'm hoping like I hope they see that he had his mind set on it. Like it may seem like I wanted him to but I didn't at all you know I loved him *like I read this thing online where it said if u agree with the person, then it makes them realize how stupid they're being and they'll stop but it didn't work* and I just idk I hope that the cops don't see it that way like I didn't bully him at all or anything. So you don't think they'll tell his family? (emphasis added)

Even on the day that it was known Conrad was dead, and for over two months after that, Michelle continued to send texts to Conrad's phone, writing to him as if he were still alive, and in one such text, sent shortly before she sent the preceding text to Samantha, she made the very same point – that she was using reverse psychology:

7/21, 10:15pm:

MICHELLE: I tried telling you not to do this every day, but every day you wouldn't listen and were just in so much pain . . . But every time I said I'd bring you to a mental hospital, you refused and I just I'm so sorry Conrad. *I read this thing online about trying to agree with the person and that would make them change their mind because they see how stupid they're being. But it didn't work for you and I did it for too long* . . . But you fucking did it and I'm so sorry I didn't save you. I tried so hard I loved you so much. You'll forever be in my heart Conrad (emphasis added)

The prosecutor dismissed Michelle's explanation that she was using reverse psychology as a self-serving lie Ms. Carter concocted after she learned detectives were investigating the case – and perhaps that is true. But the text of June 29 indicates that even before Conrad had died she had thought about encouraging him to attempt suicide, as a tactic to get him help. While that tactic seems foolish, Ms. Carter had tried more obvious strategies of being supportive, but nothing helped – Conrad was still depressed and suicidal.

Ms. Carter's intentions may be unclear – does she really want Conrad to die, though with the benevolent motive that he would be happier by ending his suffering? Does she want him to hurt himself enough that he will be hospitalized and receive treatment? Is she using reverse psychology? But her strategy in Conrad's last week is clear, marked by a shift that is apparent in the middle of the following text exchange. From that point on, Michelle, perhaps defeated and convinced that Conrad "can't live this way anymore," no longer tries to dissuade him and consistently encourages him to commit suicide and offers advice about how to do so:

7/7/14, 9:11pm:

CONRAD: I've been crying for the last hour

MICHELLE: Babe why talk to me? [her meaning probably is: babe, why? Talk to me!]

CONRAD: I hate myself so much. I can't take it.

MICHELLE: I hate seeing you this way. I want to help you but I know that my help doesn't work.

CONRAD: I'm dying on the inside . . . I'm having a complete panic attack I can't stop shaking.

MICHELLE: Close your eyes and breathe

CONRAD: I just don't see anything positive . . . everything's negative

MICHELLE: So what are you gonna do? Because you can't live this way anymore

CONRAD: If you were in my position, honestly what would you do

MICHELLE: I would get help. That's just me tho

CONRAD: Well it's too late I already gave up

MICHELLE: Ohhh okay well I'd do the CO [carbon monoxide] . . . But next I'd try the bag or hanging. . .

[Conrad then expresses doubts about getting a CO tank]

MICHELLE: Well there's more ways to make CO. Google ways to make it.

7 minutes later:

CONRAD: omg

MICHELLE: What

CONRAD: portable generator that's it. . .

MICHELLE: and take some benedryls just in case

CONRAD: See I knew you would help me find a better way. . .

7/9/14, 6:50pm:
MICHELLE: DO YOU HAVE THE GENERATOR?
CONRAD: not yet lol
MICHELLE: WELL WHEN ARE YOU GETTING IT
MICHELLE: You better not be bull sh*ting me and saying you're gonna do this and then purposely get caught

On July 11, Michelle tries to alleviate Conrad's concerns about how his family would feel once he was gone:

7/11/14, 6:59pm:
CONRAD: . . . I have a bad feeling tht this is gonna create a lot of depression between my parents/sisters. . .
MICHELLE: I think your parents know you're in a really bad place. Im not saying they want you to do it, but I honestly feel like they can except it. They know there's nothing they can do, they've tried helping . . . But there's a point that comes where there isn't anything anyone can do to save you . . . You said you're mom saw the suicide thing on your computer and she didn't say anything. I think she knows it's on your mind and she's prepared for it . . . Everyone will be sad for a while . . . I think they will understand and accept it. They'll always carry u in their hearts

[She refers to an incident they discuss in texts of 7/4/14, 9:31pm: Conrad's mother saw his laptop when it was landed on a webpage about suicide methods. Conrad said she "looked right at it" and "definitely saw it," but ignored it. He adds that he was "so shocked that she didn't ask me about it," because it was in large lettering. Michelle then suggests his mom realizes she can't stop Conrad, and is okay with it.]

Finally, shortly before Conrad's death they had this series of exchanges, widely reported by the news media:

7/12/14, 4:28am:
CONRAD: I really don't know what I'm waiting for . . . but I have everything lined up
MICHELLE: . . . You keep pushing it off and you say you'll do it but u never do. Its always gonna be that way if u don't take action . . . You're just making it harder on yourself by pushing it off, you just have to do it . . . Do u wanna do it now?
CONRAD: Is it too late? . . . I'm gonna go back to sleep, love you I'll text you tomorrow
MICHELLE: No? Its probably the best time now because everyone's sleeping. Just go somewhere in your truck. . .

10:28am:

MICHELLE: You just need to do it Conrad or I'm gonna get you help . . . If you want it as bad as you say you do it's time to do it today

CONRAD: Okay I'm gonna do it today

MICHELLE: Do you promise

CONRAD: I promise babe . . . I have to now

MICHELLE: Like right now?

CONRAD: where do I go? :(

MICHELLE: And u can't break a promise. And just go in a quiet parking lot or something. . .

6:20pm:

CONRAD: Leavin now

MICHELLE: OK you can do this

6:25pm:

CONRAD: Almost there

6:28pm:

MICHELLE: Okay

9:19pm:

MICHELLE: Please answer me . . . I'm scared are you okay? I love you please answer

Between 6:28pm and 7:58pm, Michelle's phone connected to Conrad's twice: from 6:28 to 7:10, and from 7:12 to 7:58. Phone records also indicate that Michelle called Conrad's number 28 times that evening after 7:58pm.[7] We know of the conversation during the two times they connected from a text Michelle sent to her friend Samantha over two months later, on September 15, 2014, at 8:24pm. Parts of this text suggest that Michelle directed Conrad to kill himself. A transcript of carefully selected portions of the text was broadcast nationally by ABC in an episode of *20/20* about the Carter case:

> I could have stopped it. I was the one on the phone with him and he got out of the car because [it] was working and he got scared and I fucken *told him to get back in* . . . I could have stopped him but I fucken didn't and all I had to say was I love you . . . and he'd still be here . . . I could go to jail.[8]

7 Baron, "The Girl from Plainville," pp. 130–1.

8 "Can Words Kill," *ABC's 20/20*, broadcast August 4, 2017, my emphasis. The complete text exchanges between Michelle and Samantha are available online at https://htv-prod-media.s3.amazonaws.com/files/sam-boardman-1497289698.pdf.

This sentence – 'I . . . told him to get back in' – was seized on by prosecutors and Roy's family as evidence that Michelle caused Conrad's death. We must recall that this is an account of what Michelle said two months after the fact, and not a transcript of her actual spoken words. 'Get back in' may sound like a command. But we don't know what words Michelle actually used or in what tone.

In ABC's excerpt of the September 15 text, Ms. Carter begins by saying she could have stopped Conrad; she implies the same thing in a text she sent to Samantha on July 12, at 8pm, shortly after she had disconnected with Conrad on the phone after her second call to him that evening: "there was a loud noise like a motor and I heard moaning like someone was in pain and he wouldn't answer . . . I stayed on the phone for like 20 minutes and that's all I heard. I think he just killed himself. I'm so fucken stupid . . . I should have stopped him."

Yet it isn't clear that Michelle thought that she really did have the power to determine what Conrad would do. In another part of the September 15 text to Samantha that was not reported by ABC, she expresses a mixture of thoughts, sometimes conflicting. She says she is sure she could *not* change Conrad's mind about dying, and that she acted in his best interest, as he was suffering so much:

9/15/14, 8:24–8:32pm:

MICHELLE: I couldn't have him live that way . . . I wouldn't let him. And therapy didn't help him . . . [W]hatever I said I knew I couldn't change his mind – to him it seemed like I was okay with his dying but I wasn't. Like, I didn't think he was actually going to do it . . . But you're right. He was just going to do it another time . . . I know he's finally happy. I told him it was okay to do it because he was miserable . . . and I just couldn't stand to see him like that anymore. I told him he'd be free and happy in heaven.

Of course these words are also an account two months later of what Michelle recalls saying – we don't know what she actually said over the phone.

There is a significant difference between Michelle's suggesting to Conrad ways to die while he is in the safety of his own home and the two are filling their time by texting each other, and her urging him on as he is driving to a parking lot with a water pump in his truck to generate CO, or telling him to get back in the truck as it fills with poisonous gas. It would be hard to believe that Ms. Carter would say 'get back in' as a tactic of reverse psychology or an attempt to get Conrad to a hospital where he could receive treatment. But it also seems clear from the weight of evidence of her texts that if her intention at this point was to urge him to make a successful suicide attempt, her motive was for him to end his suffering and be 'happy in heaven'.

There is some doubt as to whether Michelle's telling Conrad to 'get back in' *could* have been the proximate or immediate cause of his death, leaving aside the issue I will address in chapter 3 of whether her saying 'get back in' would have overborne Conrad's will. The exact circumstances of Conrad's death are contested. Conrad's body was discovered by police in his truck, which was parked in the lot of a K-Mart in Fairhaven, Massachusetts, on the afternoon of Sunday, July 13, and Conrad died either on the evening of July 12 or July 13. According to a journalist's account of the trial, the prosecutor, Katie Rayburn, argued that Conrad must have died during the second of the two calls Michelle placed on July 12, which started at 7:12pm and was disconnected at 7:58pm, using the logic that it takes 15 minutes to die from carbon monoxide poisoning and Conrad's phone was recovered with a dead battery.[9] Michelle had said that she stayed on the phone for 20 minutes with no response from Conrad, and heard a motor running the entire time. The prosecutor assumes that Conrad had died while Michelle was still connected, hearing his moans and the sound of something like a motor, and then his phone battery died at 7:58, ending the connection. But if it was so obvious he died before 7:58, why would Michelle frantically call Conrad 28 times after 7:58, and text him that she was scared, and ask if he was okay?

There is another theory regarding what happened. According to an article in a local newspaper, *South Coast Today*, published on January 23, 2017, Carter's attorney Joseph Cataldo indicated that the Fairhaven police checked the area of K-Mart around 3am on July 13 and did not find Conrad's pickup truck. He speculates that if Roy's truck was not in the parking lot 8 ½ hours after Carter's last contact with him, then Conrad might have driven around for some time before deciding to kill himself. That could mean that Ms. Carter's words 'get back in' did not immediately induce Conrad to commit suicide. Of course it could just mean that the police did not notice Conrad's truck during their 3am check.

Michelle was charged with involuntary manslaughter and chose a bench rather than a jury trial. The prosecutor argued that she had a motive – to get attention and sympathy from her peers – and insisted that one can commit a crime through mere words. She told the court that it didn't matter that Conrad had attempted suicide before and continued to research it, because "every day, we get a new opportunity to start again."[10] In Michelle's defense, a psychiatrist testified that Carter was on anti-depressants, tried to dissuade

9 Baron, "The Girl from Plainville," p. 130.
10 Baron, "The Girl from Plainville," p. 130.

Conrad from suicide for years, but broke under his pressure. On June 16, 2017, Judge Moniz found Carter guilty of involuntary manslaughter. In his oral explanation of his decision, he notes that she was aware of the toxic environment in the truck and must have known that if Conrad got back in, he would die. He infers that Ms. Carter wanted Conrad dead, and that her words caused him to get into the truck, which then created a duty for her to seek assistance, which she did not do.[11] Although the law allows a maximum prison term of 20 years, he sentenced her to 15 months in prison followed by probation and released her until after the appeal was concluded. On June 29, 2018, Carter's attorneys filed an appeal in the state's highest court, arguing that she was not responsible for Roy's death and that convicting her violates her due process and First Amendment rights.[12] "In February of 2019, the Supreme Judicial Court of Massachusetts unanimously upheld the conviction and Ms. Carter began serving her prison sentence."

Four underlying issues

Did Ms. Carter's words kill Conrad, and should she be punished for speaking them? In the rest of this book I present the case that she should not be punished, by turning to some fundamental issues of political, moral, and legal theory that the case raises.

Privacy

Michelle and Conrad engaged in numerous private conversations through texting and phone calls in which they shared their innermost thoughts. These conversations were made public in the course of criminal justice proceedings. Should this intimate material have been aired publicly, or should it have remained private, as it was intended to be? In chapter 2 I present the case that Michelle could reasonably expect it to have remained private. If we allow the public exposure of such information in this case, we create a precedent for future cases, and this is likely to make us hesitant to express ourselves freely even in private, and make personal, trusting relations harder to build. Privacy provides a space in which we can be free from moral judgments and shaming by the public.

But while privacy is valuable, it must not be a shield for harmful conduct or crime. For example, we should reasonably expect privacy in our sexual

11 There is no written transcript, but the video is available at https://perma.cc/NK7N-8ARM.

12 Jeremy Fox, "Michelle Carter Appeals Conviction for Encouraging Boyfriend's Suicide," *Boston Globe* (July 1, 2018).

activities in our home, but not if we are committing rape. We must weigh privacy interests against legitimate interests the public may have in exposing potential wrongdoing and punishing the guilty. Whether Ms. Carter's legitimate privacy interest is outweighed by competing interests depends on whether she may have caused harm with her words (chapter 3), and on the public interest in legally punishing her (chapters 4 and 5).

Causation and coercion

In chapter 3 I present the case that Ms. Carter was not the legally relevant cause of Conrad's death. To be legally responsible she would have had to violate some law. Massachusetts has no law against assisting or encouraging suicide, and so prosecutors instead relied on its law against involuntary manslaughter. There are two paths to manslaughter in Massachusetts: by omission (failing to intervene where one had a duty to); and by commission (causing harm through reckless action). I present the case that Ms. Carter did not commit manslaughter by omission as she had no legal duty to intervene; and she did not commit manslaughter by commission as she did not cause Conrad's death by coercing him.

Punishment

Ms. Carter and Conrad had a legitimate interest in keeping private their deeply personal text exchanges and phone conversations. But their legitimate privacy interests can give way if there is a compelling public interest in exposing this information. Exposing their private conversations after the suicide could not bring Conrad back; the primary public interest would be to determine if Ms. Carter was responsible for Conrad's death and, if she was, to punish her. In evaluating the force of this public interest, we need to consider what would be gained by punishing Ms. Carter. In chapter 4 I ask what purposes are served by punishing people generally – why do we have the practice of punishment? – so that we can see if those purposes would be served by punishing Ms. Carter. I present the case that we should not legally punish Ms. Carter on either of the two leading accounts of why we punish: retributive and utilitarian.

Suicide laws

The texts between Michelle and Conrad revealed that Conrad was at times profoundly unhappy and had attempted suicide before. Ms. Carter expressed concern, and after years of encouraging him to seek help, she appears to have become frustrated, and may have sincerely reached the point of believing Conrad would be happier in heaven. If so, then in encouraging him to kill himself, and even saying ‘get back in’ the truck, did she act badly? Is encouraging or assisting suicide always wrong, and should doing so be illegal? Ms. Carter might have deserved punishment if Massachusetts had a law that prohibited encouraging or assisting suicide, but it did not. And in chapter 5 I will present the case that there should be no such law. Some people support laws prohibiting suicide or its encouragement because they regard human life as sacrosanct; they may believe that our lives are not ours to take away because we are accountable to a higher power. But others may be skeptical of that view, regarding it as rooted in a religious or philosophical commitment they do not share; they may instead defend the right of individuals to make decisions about their lives for themselves. The issue of whether there should be laws against suicide or its encouragement forces us to address a more fundamental question of political theory: should the state use its coercive powers – including the power to punish – to impose one set of beliefs on those who do not share them?

2 Privacy

The privacy issue

Michelle Carter and Conrad Roy engaged in numerous private conversations through texting and phone calls in which they shared their innermost thoughts. They appear to have expected their conversations to remain private:

6/29/14, 7:38pm:

CONRAD: and the only way id hate you is if you told people about this. U hear me?

MICHELLE: I'm not gonna tell anyone. . .

7/8/14, 10:19am:

MICHELLE: I can't stay up past midnight anymore because my mom's mad. . .

CONRAD: How does she know

MICHELLE: She looks it up on our phone info

CONRAD: Does she read your texts

MICHELLE: Our family shares an account so she can look at everyone's stuff. She can't read the messages just sees what time they were sent and received

7/12/14, 5:17pm:

MICHELLE: Did you delete the messages?

CONRAD: Yes but ur gonna keep messaging me?

MICHELLE: I will until you turn on the generator

The texts became widely available after being introduced into the public record as evidence in the criminal proceedings against Ms. Carter. The question of whether Ms. Carter should be punished for causing Conrad to kill himself would never have been raised were it not for her texts; for example, the only way we know that Michelle told Conrad to 'get back in' his poison-filled truck was through Ms. Carter's text to her friend Samantha. I begin to address the question of whether Ms. Carter should be punished by turning to the privacy issue the case raises: should the texts have been made available in the first place? Don't we need to respect the sanctity of private conversations?

I will present the case that the texts should have been kept private. Exposing such material to the public can chill speech and make personal, trusting relations harder to build. Privacy provides a valuable space in which we can act without fear of being morally judged and publicly shamed. But I present only a 'prima facie' case. In moral philosophy the term 'prima facie' is used with respect to obligations. For example, we say there is a prima facie obligation to keep promises, meaning that when one makes a promise one has good reasons to keep it; but sometimes we ought not to do what we have an obligation to do. Prima facie obligations can be outweighed by other considerations. If I promised I would give a guest lecture in a colleague's class next Tuesday, I have a prima facie obligation to do so, but if in the meantime a loved one died and next Tuesday is the funeral, then I have a more compelling reason not to do what I have a prima facie obligation to do. In saying there is a prima facie case for keeping the texts private, I mean there are strong reasons to do so, but there may be more compelling reasons for exposing the texts that would override the reasons to keep them private. The state may have an interest in exposing private information if it is likely to uncover criminal conduct, an interest that conceivably could outweigh the interest in privacy. The state would not have such an interest if Ms. Carter could not plausibly be thought to have caused Conrad's death, or if we think that encouraging suicide should not be a crime, or if punishing her would serve little purpose, and so before settling the question of whether the texts ought to have been kept private we need to address these issues, which I do in the ensuing chapters.

The question of whether the texts should have remained private might seem moot because according to Fourth Amendment law police had every right to acquire them. The Fourth Amendment of the U.S. Constitution says "the right of the people to be secure in their persons, houses, papers, and effects, against unreasonable searches and seizures, shall not be violated, and no Warrants shall issue, but upon probable cause." It prohibits police from conducting "unreasonable searches," the operative term being 'unreasonable': even without a warrant, police can look for evidence of a crime so long as their search is reasonable. If someone is foolish enough to commit a crime on a public street in plain view of others, it would not be unreasonable for the police to observe them, and to do so they would not need a search warrant. (This is the 'plain view principle'.) Or if I give a friend pictures of me vandalizing a statue in my neighbor's backyard that I find offensive, and my friend betrays my trust and hands them over to the police, in examining the pictures the police have not conducted an unreasonable search. Warrants are required only when a search would otherwise be unreasonable. The Supreme Court has defined an unreasonable search to be a search that violates a reasonable expectation of privacy. I can't reasonably expect privacy in what I do or say if it is visible or audible to others in a public place, or in the pictures I shared with a friend who then betrays me. But if I say things in such a way that I can reasonably expect my words to remain private, to find out what I said police must get a warrant from a neutral magistrate by showing that they have probable cause to think the search will yield evidence of a crime. Later in this chapter I will argue that despite some court opinions suggesting otherwise, individuals like Michelle can reasonably expect privacy in their texts. But that might not seem to matter in the Carter case, because police had a search warrant.

Before they obtained the warrant, police acquired Conrad's phone and laptop when his father voluntarily handed them over to the police and gave them the passwords he had found in Conrad's journal.[1] If a private citizen acquires possible evidence of a crime, even by stealth, they can hand it over to the police, who can examine the evidence without a warrant. For example, if I commit a burglary and send a letter to my girlfriend instructing her to lie to the police by making up an alibi, but the letter is retrieved from my girlfriend's mailbox by her mother, who reads it and hands it over to the police, police don't need a search warrant to read the letter: they did not conduct a search, the mother did; and the Fourth Amendment does not prohibit citizens from conducting unreasonable 'private searches'; it constrains only state actors like the police.[2]

Conrad's death had originally been ruled a suicide, which is not a crime in Massachusetts or anywhere else in the United States.[3] But unattended deaths are routinely investigated in the state. When police gained access to Conrad's phone and the texts Michelle sent, they concluded that Michelle may have unduly pressured Conrad to kill himself. While there is no law in Massachusetts against encouraging or even assisting in a suicide, either, its law against involuntary manslaughter makes it a crime to cause another's

1 Jesse Baron, "The Girl from Plainville," *Esquire* (October 2017), p. 102.

2 The example is based loosely on *State v. Martinez*, 221 Ariz. 383 (2009). On private searches see also *Commonwealth v. Kean*, 556 A.2d 374 (1989).

3 Catherine Shaffer, "Criminal Liability for Assisting Suicide," *Columbia Law Review* 86(2):348–76 (1986); at p. 348.

death through reckless conduct. Police were granted a warrant to search Ms. Carter's laptop and phone, and to obtain transcripts of her texts.[4] The Fourth Amendment makes this possible by allowing police access to evidence that they have reasonable grounds to believe is relevant in solving a crime – even if it is information in which individuals can reasonably expect privacy – if they have a search warrant.

But even though police had a valid search warrant, a case still can be made that Ms. Carter's texts should have remained private, for the following reason. Police and prosecutors have discretion over whether to pursue cases in which it is unclear that a crime was committed. In Massachusetts a charge of involuntary manslaughter in a suicide case would be highly unusual, and Ms. Carter may have been the first person in the state to be convicted of killing someone on the basis of uttering words of encouragement.[5] Considering also that this was not the first time Conrad had attempted suicide, and that it might be difficult to establish that his death was caused by Michelle, the district attorney could have reasonably decided not to pursue a case against Ms. Carter, especially as putting her on trial would have damaging implications for the freedom of speech and privacy and might accomplish little in terms of making society safer. Prosecutors pursued the case, but we still are left with the normative or policy issue of whether they ought to have. Is punishing those who encourage suicide worth the intrusion upon privacy that would be needed to uncover a potential crime?

The prima facie case for privacy

I now present the case that both Michelle and Conrad had a legitimate interest in privacy: they had a legitimate interest in controlling who had access to their innermost thoughts so that those thoughts remained just between the two of them. In saying they had an interest in privacy, I mean that they had more than merely a desire for privacy. If I have an interest in something, it is important to my welfare, whereas something I merely desire may not be.[6] In saying that their interest in privacy was *legitimate*, I mean that their subjective expectation of privacy was objectively reasonable. If John inhales PCP in the public area of a public restroom, he may well subjectively expect privacy thanks to PCP's hallucinogenic effects, but his expectation

4 See Baron, "The Girl from Plainville," pp. 102–3.

5 Brief of Amici Curiae ACLU, in *Carter v. Commonwealth*, SJC-12502 (September 2018), p. 1.

6 See Mark Tunick, *Balancing Privacy and Free Speech* (London: Routledge, 2015), pp. 131–2; and Joel Feinberg, *Harm to Others* (New York: Oxford University Press, 1984), p. 32.

is objectively unreasonable since he is in plain view of anyone who happens to be there. He desires privacy, and even has an interest in privacy because without privacy he is likely to be arrested. But his desire for privacy is misplaced, and his interest is not legitimate.

Some courts have ruled that once we send a text, we can no longer expect privacy because the recipient might then share the text with others. But I will argue that just as we can reasonably expect privacy in our phone conversations, we can reasonably expect privacy in our texts.

The value of privacy

Michelle and Conrad have an interest in privacy if privacy is important to their welfare. How is privacy valuable to them? How is it important to their welfare?

Privacy would be valuable for PCP-inhaling John by letting him avoid prison. It would let individuals plan their crimes together without being detected. But it would be a mistake to think that privacy is valuable just to criminals.

One reason privacy is valuable is that it allows us to form and develop intimate relationships. Charles Fried argues that without privacy, "respect, love, friendship and trust" are "simply inconceivable": "Privacy creates the moral capital which we spend in friendship and love."[7] To feel the force of his argument, imagine that every word we spoke or wrote was stored online and publicly accessible by using an internet search engine. We would have no control over whom we share information with. The problem in this scenario is not just that we might be too embarrassed to whisper sweet nothings to our loved ones because anybody else could hear. We couldn't share so much more with them: our secrets, our fantasies, or our unconventional thoughts; we couldn't express our criticism of those we fear; nor could we talk about our loved ones with other people whom we trust and consult for advice. Not only would we lose one of the strongest bonds between friends and lovers – the ability to selectively disclose our inner thoughts and feelings – but insofar as those very thoughts and feelings define who we are, we risk losing ourselves. Aware that we would be judged by prevailing social norms, we might succumb to the pressure to say whatever will please the majority. John Stuart Mill eloquently expressed his fears about the conforming power of public opinion in *On Liberty*, though he did not emphasize how important privacy is as a weapon against this threat.

7 Charles Fried, "Privacy," in Schoeman, ed., *Philosophical Dimensions of Privacy* (New York: Cambridge University Press, 1984), pp. 203–22; at pp. 205, 211.

Privacy is also valuable to members of minority cultures or religious groups that are threatening to the majority. While ideally they should be able to freely exercise their religion or partake in their cultural practices in public, doing so might create tensions with the majority. Having a private space to practice their customs or religion at least lets them coexist with the majority. Michael Walzer gives the example of how 19th-century German Jews said "German in the street, Jewish at home." Being able to retreat to a protected private sphere, he argues, is a condition of toleration – though as his example eerily reminds us, it doesn't guarantee toleration.[8] Privacy can help us form bonds with others we have an affinity for, be they friends, or those who share our culture, political views, religion, or rejection of religion.

A related account of why privacy is important to our welfare is that it lets us express and be ourselves without being defined, judged, and punished for thoughts or behavior that might not truly represent all that we are. The idea that privacy lets us avoid unjust punishment is one I have emphasized in my previous work, and draws on an important argument laid out by Jeffrey Rosen.

Rosen presents the 'synecdoche' argument. A synecdoche is a figure of speech where a part is taken to represent the whole. If pieces of information about us are publicized, such as the books we read or videos we stream, they may be used to represent whom we really are, unfairly reducing or stereotyping us based on a 'snippet'. Privacy, in restricting access to these snippets, protects us from being simplified and judged out of context.[9]

Rosen provides the example of Clarence Thomas. When he was nominated to be a Supreme Court Justice, bits of information about him were publicized, such as that he rented pornographic videos and made unwelcome and inappropriate remarks with distinct sexual overtones to his employee at the time, Anita Hill; this almost led to the squelching of his nomination. Rosen agrees with Thomas's complaint that .2% of him was being used to destroy him (143).

One might object: what if the inappropriate comments Justice Thomas allegedly made reveal something core about his character that would be relevant to his suitability as a Supreme Court Justice? The act of theft may reflect just .2% of an individual's activity during the year, but shouldn't they be judged for that snippet of their life? How do we know these judgments are incorrect – don't we need more information to know?

8 Michael Walzer, *On Toleration* (New Haven: Yale University Press, 1997), p. 26.
9 Jeffrey Rosen, *The Unwanted Gaze* (New York: Random House, 2000), pp. 20, 223.

Rosen is aware of these objections and responds in a few ways. First, he is not saying that we should never judge others; on the contrary, he suggests there is even a "right to misjudge" (117). But society's interests in accessing information and judging others must be balanced against the interest in privacy, even of those suspected of wrongdoing. Where it is important to have information in particular circumstances, access should be made available. But protections should be in place so that snippets of private information that could be used to unfairly characterize us are not needlessly released. He proposes that we have virtual 'backstage spaces' that are immune from surveillance (208); and where we need access to sensitive information about someone he suggests measures such as using a privacy master to ensure that information is made known only for very narrowly defined and legitimate purposes, and only to those with a need to know (181).

One way to avoid misjudging someone based on snippets is to gather even more information about them so that we are more likely to see the person's true character – which would require even greater intrusions upon privacy. Rosen doesn't support that solution in part because he is skeptical that there is a true self to find. We "display different characters in different contexts," depending on whom we are interacting with. Rosen notes that he behaves in one way when interacting with students, in other ways with his family, or with close friends, and wears still a different public mask when he visits his drycleaner. Rosen argues, "If these masks were to be violently torn away, as Clarence Thomas's ordeal shows, what would be exposed is not my true self but the spectacle of a wounded and defenseless man" (210).

But what if the wounded man deserves some blame? Whereas Rosen suggests that people like Clarence Thomas shouldn't be judged for past indiscretions that are best left private, there are times when masks hide blameworthy conduct for which one ought to be held accountable – a proposition Rosen surely agrees with. We need to distinguish the state's interest in punishing those who violate the law – or other compelling interests the state may have, such as ensuring Supreme Court nominees are beyond reproach – from other public interests in uncovering information that are not compelling enough to justify intrusions upon privacy.

In my prior work on privacy I try to draw such a distinction by differentiating the state's interest in legal punishment from the public's less compelling interest in meting out non-legal punishment.[10] Non-legal punishment, or 'moral punishment', involves shaming or reproaching someone because we think they acted badly. There are problems with the very practice of moral punishment that should make us cautious about engaging in it. There

10 Mark Tunick, "Privacy and Punishment," *Social Theory and Practice* 39(4):634–68 (2013).

are no clear, agreed-upon standards for deciding whether someone acted badly; there is no formal process the accused can rely on to defend themselves; and there is no guarantee that an appropriate amount of punishment will be meted out. Given the looseness of standards and lack of due process, there is a heightened risk that the dangers that Rosen warns us about will be realized: that people will judge others unfairly based on snippets or sound bites. The resulting damage to one's reputation can be devastating. People have committed suicide because they could not bear being judged.[11] One of the dangers endemic to moral as opposed to legal punishment is that it is likely to be excessive when in response to widely publicized conduct. Legal punishment is meted out only by the state, once for each conviction, ideally in an amount proportional to the seriousness of the offense; but an individual whose conduct is made widely known might receive moral punishment from multiple people and for as long as people are aware of the alleged misconduct, which, in our internet age, can be a lifetime, because information is archived and easily accessed through search engines. Non-legal or moral punishment is incompatible with the project of issuing a coordinated response and is unlikely to be proportionate.[12]

There are legitimate interests in sharing information so that people can assess each other's character. Gossip, for example, serves a useful social function in helping people decide whom they should trust and whom they should avoid; and economists rightly point to the value of having information about those we may do business with. Morally taking someone to task can have salutary deterrent and reformative effects; and the interest in judging a nominee for the Supreme Court or other public figures can be particularly weighty. But gossip can be unreliable and harmful.

Moral punishment may be more reliable and effective when inflicted by someone who has close ties to the person they punish, already knows a good deal about them, and is less likely to judge based on snippets. They are also less likely to create a risk of over-punishment insofar as their punishment remains private. To illustrate the distinction between non-legal punishment that is private and that which is public, consider the case of 'Cannibal Cop'. Gilberto Valle, a New York City police officer, was frequenting online chatrooms dedicated to cannibalism, where he and anonymous strangers would exchange fantasies about abducting, killing, and eating women. He had a

11 See Tunick, *Balancing Privacy and Free Speech*, pp. 2–3, referring to the suicides of college student Tyler Clementi (when he was exposed kissing a man), and Louis Conradt (a Texas assistant district attorney who killed himself when *Dateline NBC* cameras approached his home because he had engaged in sexually explicit online chat with a decoy posing as an underage teen).

12 Tunick, "Privacy and Punishment," p. 649.

substantial interest in keeping his fantasies private. His wife had a substantial interest in finding out about the dark inner thoughts of her husband, even though her snooping through the laptop he used could breach the mutual trust they may have had in each other. Valle's wife's interest in knowing his inner thoughts to see whether he is really the person she thought she married may outweigh his privacy interest, and the private punishment she inflicted by leaving him is not excessive. But after she called in the FBI, and a prosecutor charged Valle with conspiracy to kidnap, he received widespread public blame and scorn even though he was eventually acquitted in the courtroom. Valle had no prior history of violating any laws or posing a threat, and the public, unlike Valle's wife, had no legitimate need to know about his fantasies. The police would need to know only if his fantasies would probably translate into harmful action.[13]

The space privacy provides so that we can express ourselves to those we trust without being unfairly judged and unjustly punished by the public is especially valuable for people in intimate relations. Family members and intimate friends need the ability to get mad at each other, say things they don't mean, joke, or vent their anger, without fearing that their words will be used against them in a courtroom or the court of public opinion. But privacy must not be a shield for harmful conduct. We should generally respect the privacy of families but not when it would cloak domestic violence or child abuse. Privacy is always something we must balance against competing interests.

Michelle's and Conrad's interest in privacy is legitimate

Michelle and Conrad had an interest in keeping their text exchanges private. Michelle has been vilified on the basis of carefully edited snippets that present her as a villain. Many of her other texts paint a different picture, of a teenage girl who cared for and tried to help her troubled friend, got frustrated, and may have genuinely believed suicide was his only way to end his misery. Michelle had an interest in not being judged based on snippets. Earlier I asserted that Michelle's and Conrad's interest was *legitimate*, by which I meant they had an objectively reasonable expectation and not a misplaced desire that their texts would stay just between themselves. I now defend that claim.

13 See Mark Tunick, "Brain Privacy and the Case of Cannibal Cop," *Res Publica* 23(2):179–96 (2017).

Reasonable expectations of privacy

When we walk down a busy street, talking to a friend, it would be unreasonable to expect others to look away or cover their ears. If we want our conversation to be private we should whisper or speak in code; if we don't want others to see us together, we should wear good disguises. But we should not have to retreat to a windowless, soundproof basement to have private conversations. We can reasonably expect privacy if what we do or say is not in plain view or earshot of anyone who can see or hear us from a vantage point where they have a right to be. (This is a corollary of the 'plain view principle'.) If what we say could be observed by someone only if they use impermissible means of observation such as a listening device, or are at a vantage point where they have no right to be, we have a reasonable expectation of privacy in our words.[14]

Certain methods of observation have been deemed by courts to be impermissible when used without a warrant. For example, government may not listen in on phone conversations without a warrant. In the landmark case of *Katz v. United States*, Mr. Katz was in a public phone booth transmitting wagering information, in violation of federal law. Without a warrant, federal agents used a listening device to amplify the words Katz spoke, heard him incriminate himself, and arrested him. Katz claimed that his conviction should be reversed because the evidence against him was obtained in violation of the Fourth Amendment. The Court agreed, holding that when Katz "shuts the door behind him, and pays the toll," he can reasonably expect privacy. To listen in, police needed a search warrant.[15]

Suppose two people text each other to plot a crime. They have a privacy interest in keeping their scheme from being known to the police, and in the next section I argue that we can reasonably expect privacy in our texts just as Katz could reasonably expect privacy in his phone call. One might think, though, that even if we generally can, their interest can't be legitimate because people plotting crimes shouldn't have a right to privacy. Arnold Loewy argues that reasonable expectations of privacy should refer to the expectations "which should be accorded to an innocent person."[16] But rather than say that, we should say the plotting couple do have a legitimate interest in privacy, but that interest may be outweighed by the state's interest in preventing crime. We have a legitimate interest in

14 See Tunick, *Balancing Privacy and Free Speech*, p. 65.

15 389 U.S. 347, 352 (1967).

16 Cf. Arnold Loewy, "The Fourth Amendment as a Device for Protecting the Innocent," *Michigan Law Review* 81(5):1229–72 (1983); at p. 1249.

privacy if we can reasonably expect privacy, and whether we can depends only on whether what we do or say is in plain view or earshot of those using permissible means of observation from a vantage point they have a right to assume. It will depend, for example, on whether we are keeping our thoughts hidden in a locked diary or publishing them in a public blog; or whether we are whispering them to a trusted loved one or shouting them through an amplifier in Central Park. Whether our privacy interest is legitimate does *not* depend on what it is we want to keep private. Regardless of whether the two people discussing a crime are serious or just fantasizing or play acting, they have a legitimate interest in privacy. But if they are serious, that interest might be outweighed by a competing interest in preventing harm. We must keep in mind that the interest in preventing crime isn't necessarily sufficient to outweigh the interest in privacy: Katz, after all, was violating a federal law, but the Supreme Court held that he nevertheless had a right to privacy.

Reasonable expectations of privacy in texts

The question we now must ask is whether people like Michelle and Conrad can reasonably expect privacy in their texts. To address this, it is helpful to think about the nature of texting.

Prior to texting and online chats, there would be no permanent record of a conversation unless it was recorded. An exchange of letters could leave a permanent record, but I distinguish an exchange of letters from a *conversation* in which the two parties immediately respond back and forth, reacting to each other's words. For centuries, letters have allowed people to exchange intimate thoughts without being face to face. But even though the length of time to send a letter shortened with advances in technology, letters never could replace face to face exchanges in which you could see someone's immediate reaction and respond to it. Phone calls and texting make it possible to conduct private, intimate exchanges that approximate face to face interactions to a much greater degree.

This is not to say that letters were not empowering: one could scheme and plot, persuade, coerce, blackmail, and threaten, safely from a distance, with mere words unaccompanied by a physical presence. But letters do not allow one to engage in a genuine conversation, and this is significant because the give and take of conversations may present opportunities for moving another to action that merely writing words that are later read do not. Texts can be a functional equivalent of face to face interaction, and someone who uses texts to persuade another to commit a wrongful act might be as much of a proximate or immediate cause of the wrong as if they had physically been present, a point I will return to in chapter 3.

But if we recognize text exchanges as nearly equivalent to face to face conversations, making texts publicly available raises privacy concerns. Conversations carefully conducted out of earshot of others elicit an expectation of privacy that the *Katz* Court recognized as reasonable. If we recognize phone conversations as private, shouldn't we recognize the privacy of text exchanges? Texting arguably creates an even greater demand for privacy because texts can be archived and retrieved, unlike most phone conversations. Before the advent of texting, and had Michelle and Conrad communicated solely by phone, prosecutors would have had no case to pursue.

Some courts, however, have held that individuals cannot reasonably expect privacy in their texts. Appealing to a variation of the 'third-party doctrine', their reasoning is that you cannot expect privacy in information that you voluntarily convey to the person you text, or to a third party such as the phone service provider, since you can't control whether they will then pass this information on to others including the police. (A paradigmatic third-party doctrine case involves A calling B and in doing so voluntarily conveying that fact to a third party – such as a phone company – who then shares the information with the government. But cases in which A tells something to B and B then conveys what A said to the government have been considered third-party doctrine cases as well.)[17] However, the cases in which courts allowed police to access texts without a warrant can be distinguished from the Carter case; moreover, the third-party doctrine has been recently challenged by the U.S. Supreme Court. Before developing these points, it is important to remember that the question I'm addressing isn't whether police should have gotten a warrant to search Ms. Carter's texts – they had one. The issue is whether she and Conrad had a legitimate interest in privacy, because only if they did should we weigh that interest against competing public interests in deciding whether the police and prosecutors ought to have violated her privacy in pursuing the case against her.

In *State v. Tentoni*, a police officer found the dead body of Wayne Wilson with a fentanyl patch in his mouth that turned out to be the cause of his death. Wilson's phone was nearby, and the officer, without a search warrant, took it and retrieved text messages between Wilson and the defendant, Tentoni. In the texts, Tentoni instructs Wilson on how to get and use fentanyl patches. Based on the texts, the officer got a warrant for the phone and all text messages, and Tentoni was eventually convicted of 2nd-degree reckless homicide. A unanimous three-judge panel ruled that Tentoni had no property interest in Wilson's phone, and no control over it, and therefore had no

17 Owen Kerr treats *Hoffa v. U.S.*, discussed later, as a third-party doctrine case in "The Case for the Third-Party Doctrine," *Michigan Law Review* 107(4):561–601 (2009).

reasonable expectation of privacy in his texts to Wilson. One assumes the risk that the person one texts will disclose the texts to a third party.[18]

The *Tentoni* case might be distinguished from Carter's because Tentoni's relation with Wilson may not have been intimate and based on mutual trust, whereas the relationship between Michelle and Conrad was. One assumption underlying the third-party doctrine is that you cannot expect privacy when you reveal something to another party since you can't control what they will do with that information: the cat is out of the bag. However, people in an intimate relationship do have some assurance of confidentiality – the assurance provided by their relation of mutual trust and implicit promises that what they say stays between the two of them.

Several other court decisions similarly held that there is no reasonable expectation of privacy in texts or phone calls sent to others. But they also appear to involve people who lacked an intimate connection – co-conspirators in a crime, or co-workers. In *State v. Carle*, police found the phone of someone named Duane in a car that had been reported stolen, and saw messages on Duane's phone from the defendant, Angel, indicating Angel wanted to sell methamphetamine to Duane. Posing as Duane, an officer sent a text from Duane's phone to Angel, arranging for a drug sale. When Angel showed up to complete the transaction, the police arrested her. The Court held that Angel has no privacy interest in her texts once they are delivered to another phone.[19] In *State v. Goucher*, police answered a phone while executing a search warrant, didn't reveal they were officers, and arranged a drug deal with the caller, who was then arrested. The caller was held not to have a reasonable expectation of privacy in the call because he was willing to speak with anyone who answered at that location.[20] And in *Fetsch v. City of Roseburg*, a police employee texted about an extramarital affair he had with a subordinate, to a probationary officer he was supervising. The probationary officer then showed the texts to a higher supervisor. The court held that the employee could not reasonably expect privacy in his texts, even though he had asked the probationary officer to keep them secret, as he could not control what the probationary officer would do with the messages.[21]

There have even been cases in which an exchange occurred between friends, or people in an intimate relationship, but still the court held there was no reasonable expectation of privacy. In *State v. Patino*, police found

18 365 Wis. 2d 211 (Ct of Appeals of Wisconsin, 2015).
19 266 Or. App. 102 (2014).
20 124 Wash. 2d 778 (1994).
21 2012 WL 6742665 (2012); not reported in F. Supp. 2d (D. Oregon).

incriminating texts sent between the defendant, Patino, and his girlfriend, Trisha, suggesting that Patino had gotten mad at Trisha's 6-year-old boy Marco and hit him. Earlier, Marco had been rushed to the hospital after Trisha found him unresponsive, and the boy died. While at the hospital, Trisha permitted the police to search her phone, after police had already viewed some incriminating messages from phones still in her apartment, and they used the texts they found to pressure Patino to confess. Rhode Island's Supreme Court ruled that Patino had no reasonable expectation of privacy in the texts he sent Trisha because he could not control whether she shared them with the police.[22] However, at the point when she did share them, any relationship of mutual trust she had with Patino was surely dissolved. And in an influential U.S. Supreme Court ruling, *Hoffa v. U.S.*, the Court held that when Jimmy Hoffa revealed incriminating information to a friend who unbeknownst to him was a government informer, Hoffa had no reasonable expectation of privacy in what he said: the Fourth Amendment doesn't protect one's "misplaced belief that a person to whom he voluntarily confides his wrongdoing will not reveal it."[23] Both cases can be distinguished from the Carter case. The *Hoffa* court speaks abstractly of the informer "prevailing upon friendship" but doesn't indicate anything more about his relationship with Hoffa. Ms. Carter's relationship with Conrad was probably more firmly rooted in mutual trust than Hoffa's relationship with his friend, who may have been more of a close business associate. And nothing happened in Michelle and Conrad's relationship that would have undermined its basis in mutual trust as happened in *State v. Patino*.

Other courts *have* recognized a reasonable expectation of privacy in texts, even between those who are not necessarily in an intimate relationship. A three-judge panel for the Missouri Court of Appeals unanimously ruled in *State v. Clampitt* that acquiring texts from a service provider violated a reasonable expectation of privacy. The court noted that "as text messaging becomes an ever-increasing substitute for the more traditional forms of communication, it follows that society expects the contents of text messages to receive the same 4th Amendment protections afforded to letters and phone calls."[24] In *State v. Bone*, acquiring the texts of a suspect in a gang-related shooting with a subpoena but not a search warrant was held to violate the Fourth Amendment. One of the leading Supreme Court precedents that invoked the third-party doctrine – *Smith v. Maryland* – ruled that one

22 93 A. 3d 40 (Sup Ct of Rhode Island, 2014). See also *U.S. v. Dunning*, 312 F. 3d 528 (1st Cir. 2002).

23 385 US 293, 302 (1966).

24 *State v. Clampitt*, 364 S.W. 3d 605 (2012).

has no reasonable expectation of privacy in the phone numbers one dials because one voluntarily gives this information to a third party – the phone company – which can then convey this information to the government. But in *Bone*, the Louisiana Court of Appeals recognized that we don't voluntarily convey the *content* of our text messages to our service provider.[25] And in *State v. Hinton*, the Supreme Court of Washington reversed a lower court ruling and held that when the police took Lee's iPhone, saw a text from the defendant Hinton, and texted back, posing as Lee, in order to set up a drug deal, they violated Hinton's reasonable expectation of privacy. The 7–4 majority noted that the content of a text message can be as intimate as the content of a phone call, and argued that while Hinton assumed the risk that the person he communicated with would betray him by telling the police – which happened in *Hoffa* – that's not what happened here. Hinton doesn't assume the risk that police will acquire Lee's phone.[26]

The *Hinton* court recognizes that if someone you trust betrays that trust, you assumed that risk. It would be problematic to say that we assume the risk that someone will betray our trust when they do so because they were coerced by the state, so we should sharpen that principle by requiring that the betrayal truly be voluntary. But only in *Fetsch* and *Patino* did the intended recipient of a text, letter, or call in fact voluntarily convey to the government what the defendant said, and in those cases either there was no basis for trust (*Fetsch*), or the trusting relationship between the parties had dissolved (*Patino*). In *Carle*, the phone with incriminating evidence was not handed over to the police but was found abandoned in a car; in *Goucher*, there was no intended recipient in particular; and in *Hoffa*, the government informant in whom Hoffa confided arguably did not hand the information over voluntarily since the reason he informed was to avoid prison.

But the *Hinton* court flatly rejected the principle that the mere possibility that the party you share information with could betray you means you cannot reasonably expect privacy in what you say to them. According to that principle, since whomever Katz spoke with on the phone could have betrayed Katz to the police, Katz cannot reasonably expect privacy in his conversation and therefore the police would be free to listen in using whatever means they please. But of course that is not what the Supreme Court held. The *Hinton* court was right to reject that principle, for enforcing it would have a dramatic chilling effect on both privacy and free speech. Since betrayal is almost always a possibility, if we enforced that principle we could never reasonably expect privacy. Because Conrad and Michelle had

25 *State v. Bone*, 107 So. 3d 49 (2012), referring to *Smith v. Maryland*, 442 U.S. 735 (1979).
26 *State v. Hinton*, 179 Wash. 2d 862, 870–5 (2014).

a trusting relationship that had not dissolved, and neither betrayed that trust by voluntarily handing over their phones or laptops to the police, we should recognize their expectation of privacy as reasonable.

Tentoni stands out because in that case, police gained access to incriminating texts when they acquired Wilson's phone after he died, just as police obtained Conrad's phone from his father after Conrad had died. The *Tentoni* court assumes that expectations of privacy are extinguished once one dies. But that, too, is a dangerous principle, for several reasons. While we are no longer around to bear the consequences of a stained reputation once we die, people close to us may bear those consequences. Second, Wilson's or Conrad's privacy is not all that is at stake when we expose their texts. Those they texted expected the exchanges to remain private. Enforcing the principle that the government may see whatever confidences we share with those who then die would have the same chilling effect as enforcing the principle that I can't expect privacy in information I share with someone who conceivably could betray my trust. Police would be able to conduct fishing expeditions whenever someone dies, without the restraints imposed by a warrant. The inconvenience of securing a warrant is unlikely to outweigh the costs to privacy if we give police unbridled access to the phones of those who just died.

Some recent Supreme Court decisions lend support to the view that we can reasonably expect privacy in our texts, though the Court has yet to decide the issue. In 2010 it considered whether the City of Ontario violated the Fourth Amendment by gaining access to the text messages of Mr. Quon, an employee who was using a city-supplied text pager. The Court assumed without deciding that Quon had a reasonable expectation of privacy in his texts, but held that because the texts were supposed to be work-related, there was a special needs exception that permitted the City to look at the text logs for purposes of seeing if Quon's monthly usage was too high.[27] More recently, in *Riley v. California*, the Court held that one can reasonably expect privacy in the content on one's smartphone. The Court compared smartphones to diaries – they contain calendars, one's internet searches, the apps one uses, and other information that can reveal a person's entire past; and so police need a warrant to search them.[28] Finally, in *Carpenter v. U.S.* the Supreme Court revisited the third-party doctrine.[29] Without a search warrant, the government obtained cell phone records for the defendant Carpenter's phone and tracked his location for over 127 days, to see if he was nearby when multiple robberies occurred. The Court declined to

27 *City of Ontario v. Quon*, 560 U.S. 746 (2010).
28 573 U.S. __ (2014).
29 *Carpenter v. U.S.*, __S.Ct.__ (June 2018).

apply *Smith*'s third-party doctrine here: what was conveyed in *Smith* – the phone numbers one dials – is less sensitive than one's location. The Court also disagreed with the claim that Carpenter voluntarily conveyed his location to his service provider, since one has no choice but to do so if one uses a cell phone.

If the Supreme Court agrees that in using my phone I don't voluntarily give the service provider free sway to share my location with others, it seems likely the Court would agree that I also do not consent to their sharing the content of my texts without a search warrant. The *Carpenter* court, however, did not address the *Hoffa* and *Hinton* question of whether we can expect privacy in what we say to another party given the possibility that they, rather than the third-party service provider, might share what we said with the government.

Balancing privacy against competing interests

Michelle had a legitimate privacy interest in her texts. But merely having a legitimate privacy interest does not mean one has a right to privacy. Privacy must be weighed against competing interests.

The need to balance

It is valuable to have a private space that is shielded from public scrutiny, but it can also be dangerous. The privacy that Walzer refers to, which enables a religious minority to exercise its religion without threatening the majority, might also allow them to physically abuse their children if that is an accepted part of their religion. Privacy shouldn't be a shield for harmful, criminal conduct.

The danger that privacy can sometimes pose, and the need to balance privacy against competing interests, is illustrated in the case of *State v. Duchow*, decided by the Supreme Court of Wisconsin.[30] A school bus driver, Brian Duchow, shouted abusively at Jacob, a 9-year-old boy with Downs Syndrome, and also slapped him. Jacob was the first student to be picked up on the bus route, and the abusive behavior took place when he and Jacob were alone on the bus with no other witnesses. Jacob has a significant speech impairment and was unable to communicate what happened, but he acted oddly, and his parents suspected that something was wrong. They put a voice-activated recorder in his backpack and it recorded Duchow making abusive statements, and the sound of slapping. Duchow was convicted of disorderly conduct and physical abuse of a child and appealed, claiming that

30 310 Wis.2d 1 (2008).

recording him violated state privacy law, which prohibits recording conversations in which one could reasonably expect privacy. Duchow claimed that he could reasonably expect privacy because he was alone with Jacob. The Wisconsin Supreme Court rejected his claim: he may have had a subjective expectation of privacy, but it was not objectively reasonable.

According to the logic of the plain view principle, Duchow perhaps should have prevailed, because what he said and did was not in plain view or earshot of anyone who could reveal it to others. The Court suggested that Jason was able to report the threatening behavior to his parents in his own way, by acting up, smashing his toys, kicking his dog, and crying at school when it was time to get on the bus. But Jason couldn't provide specific testimony that would warrant action against Duchow without the recording. If someone else would've been on the bus at the time, or if Jacob didn't have his impairment, Duchow's behavior would've been made known – or more likely, deterred. But there are compelling reasons for adopting the position the *Hinton* court took, that whether our expectations of privacy are reasonable should depend not on whether our words could conceivably be permissibly observed by others but on whether permissible means of observation were actually used; and Duchow's behavior was revealed only by the impermissible means of making a recording without his consent.

But that outcome would be impossible to stomach. To avoid it, the Court also used a 'totality of circumstances' approach. It listed factors that help determine whether one can reasonably expect to keep one's conversation private, including its volume, proximity to others, and potential for the communication to be reported – but these all favored Duchow's claim that he could expect privacy. Another factor is the place or location. Here the place was a public school bus, and the Court argued that just as teachers cannot reasonably expect privacy in what they say in their classroom, Duchow, as a school employee, could not expect privacy on the bus. That comparison is inapt, though, since teachers in a classroom are typically in plain view of many students, whereas on the bus no one was present who could convey what Duchow said and did. The Court's most convincing justification for ruling against Duchow ultimately relied on a balancing approach: "the presence of a recording device on a bus is a minor intrusion on a driver" given society's interest in ensuring safety on buses (310 Wis. 2d 1, 27). We can reach the appropriate outcome by holding that Duchow had a reasonable expectation of privacy, but his legitimate privacy interest is clearly outweighed by the state's interest in protecting Jason and exposing Duchow's criminal conduct.

Duchow illustrates how having a legitimate privacy interest, or an objectively reasonable expectation of privacy, need not mean that one should have a protected right to privacy. Privacy interests can be outweighed by competing interests. I have argued that Michelle and Conrad both have a legitimate privacy interest in their texts. Because their case stands as a precedent for future cases, the privacy interest at stake is not just theirs, but the interest similarly situated individuals may have in expressing themselves through texts, just as the privacy interest at stake in *Katz* was not just Mr. Katz's interest in not getting caught, but the public's interest in being able to have private conversations in phone booths. What countervailing interests could outweigh this privacy interest? What is gained by peering deeply into the relationship of Michelle and Conrad?

The main interest in having access to the texts would be to determine if Ms. Carter was responsible for Conrad's death and, if she was, to judge and punish her. As I indicated in the section "The value of privacy," in assessing that interest we must distinguish between the interest in moral and legal punishment.

The interest in moral punishment

By moral punishment, or what I earlier called non-legal punishment, I refer to members of the public blaming and expressing disapproval of those they believe have acted badly. I argued earlier that moral punishment can be problematic because there is no definitive standard for deciding what counts as acting badly, no due process for the accused, and no assurance that the amount of punishment meted out will be proportionate and just. There are, though, valid interests in sharing information so that people can decide whom to trust: reputations depend on this.

But as I argued earlier in discussing Rosen's 'synecdoche' argument, making fair and just moral judgments requires having more than snippets. It's easier to judge characters richly portrayed in a novel than to judge real people who are known to us only in bits and pieces: we might see them only in one role but not in the many others that make up their life. Misjudgment is inevitable.

Herman Melville illustrates the point in *Billy Budd*.[31] He presents to us the youthful and innocent sailor Billy Budd, and the serpentine, deceiving, and conniving master-at-arms, John Claggart, who, for reasons wholly obscure to Billy, has it in for him. Claggart, "a depravity according to nature," unjustly accuses Billy of plotting a mutiny, a charge that leaves Billy speechless. He impulsively strikes Claggart with a fatal blow, which requires Billy to then be put to death. The reader is given the 'inside

31 Herman Melville, *Billy Budd, Sailor (An Inside Narrative)*, eds. Harrison Hayford and Merton M. Sealts, Jr. (Chicago: University of Chicago Press, 1962).

narrative' and knows that Billy, a 'baby' and 'man-child' who cannot comprehend double meanings, was not plotting a mutiny, and that Claggart was the villain. But in the penultimate chapter, Melville shares the public account of Claggart's killing, published in a naval chronicle: Claggart discovered an incipient plot whose "ringleader was one William Budd," who vindictively stabbed Claggart. The account refers to "[t]he enormity of the crime and the extreme depravity of the criminal," whereas Claggart is depicted as "respectable and discreet." The story's narrator then notes that the preceding account "is all that hitherto has stood in human record to attest what manner of men respectively were John Claggart and Billy Budd" (Ch. 29, pp. 130–1). The legal punishment inflicted according to maritime law was severe, though it was not undeserved given that Billy was guilty of manslaughter, and it may have been necessary to quell a possible mutiny. But lacking access to the inside narrative, the chronicler got the moral judgment utterly wrong, as we are often likely to do when we morally judge without knowing all the relevant facts.

Ms. Carter has already been publicly judged. On Feb. 8, 2019, NBC aired an episode of 'Dateline' about the Carter case that was titled "Reckless," and which at one point refers to Conrad's "alleged suicide," as if to suggest he may have been murdered. ABC's nationally televised *20/20* report on the case provided a sounding board for Conrad's relatives to express their outrage at Michelle. Some of those who were interviewed portrayed Ms. Carter as a villain and expressed shock that she had the audacity to attend Conrad's wake. If the audience had access to the numerous texts in which Michelle and Conrad expressed their feelings for each other, they might have better understood why she attended. To fairly judge Ms. Carter morally, we would need access to more than the snippets of texts that ABC and other news media outlets reported. Had *Dateline*'s audience known that just before he died Conrad texted Michelle that his pain was "unbearable," they might have viewed more skeptically the assessment of Conrad's relative, who assures the viewers that "You can tell [Conrad] did not want to die." To get moral punishment right, we need to invade privacy even more. But given the limitations and risks in moral punishment – especially in its public form, as opposed to the private form that people in intimate relations might mete out on each other – the interest in doing so is not very strong, and may not even be a legitimate interest. It can be important for prospective employers to have relevant information about job applicants, or for an individual to know about the character of a potential spouse or partner. But the interest in publicly shaming Ms. Carter based on snippets that may mischaracterize her intentions and complicity, for an act – encouraging suicide – that in some circumstances is not clearly wrong, is unlikely to outweigh the privacy interest at stake. That is the case I will continue to present in the ensuing chapters.

If we start scrutinizing Conrad's interactions with Michelle to see what factors led him to commit suicide, one might argue that we should also scrutinize his relationships with others, including his family. If we are going to try to explain his suicide, shouldn't we consider the role that may have been played by his father, who reportedly punched Conrad in the face so badly five months earlier that he had to go to the hospital?[32] Shouldn't we ask why his mother saw Conrad's laptop landed on a page about how to commit suicide, yet said nothing? My point is not that his parents were to blame, only that once we start casting blame, to be just and fair we might be forced to intrude into spaces that should be protected, including the intimate space of family life. Once you start questioning me, everything I do becomes suspect and I'm put in the position of having to defend things I do that I should not have to defend. Michelle has been questioned for why she would pretend to her friend Sam that she didn't know where Conrad was on his last day, when she did know. People are deceptive for all sorts of reasons, and one shouldn't have to defend everything one says and does before the unreliable court of public opinion.

The interest in legal punishment

While the interest in moral punishment is problematic, the state has a compelling interest in discovering and punishing crime. To be sure, legal punishment can be unjust. But because of the protections built into the criminal justice system, it is not as likely to be unjust as is public, moral punishment.

But the interest in legally punishing Michelle is problematic because no law was clearly violated. The prosecutor brought charges of involuntary manslaughter that I address in the next chapter, but had the discretion not to file charges. In deciding whether that decision was supportable even though it required intrusions upon legitimate privacy interests, we need to assess the strength of the potential public interest in punishing, and this will require us to ask whether Ms. Carter could have caused harm with her words (chapter 3), what the interest in legally punishing her is if she did (chapter 4), and whether we even ought to have laws against encouraging suicide (chapter 5).

32 Barron, "The Girl from Plainville," p. 102.

3 Causation and coercion

The issue

Michelle Carter did not put the idea of suicide in Conrad Roy's head – it was there before Conrad met Michelle. It would be fair to say that Conrad was predisposed to killing himself: he struggled with bouts of depression, apparently talked with people on the internet as far away as Britain about suicide methods, and told Michelle that he had made a few prior attempts. We saw that Michelle at first tried to dissuade him. Perhaps because she got frustrated that her efforts weren't helping, in late June or early July of 2014 she began to encourage Conrad to end his life and offered advice about how to do so. Michelle texted Conrad on July 4 that carbon monoxide is the best way. A few days later, Conrad texted her that he could get a portable generator. That plan didn't work, and so Michelle gave him some further advice: go to Sears to get a generator. Conrad never did follow that advice. At Michelle's suggestion, Conrad then did a google search to learn how to rig his truck to fill with carbon monoxide. According to the prosecutors, Michelle's advice and encouragement, which we will look at in more detail in this chapter, were the impetus Conrad needed. Sometimes Michelle's persistence might be perceived as pressure. While she never threatened Conrad, she did ask him to promise he'd go through with his plans, and repeatedly said 'you just need to do it'. Most importantly, after Conrad had stepped out of the truck that was filling with poisonous gas, Michelle told him to 'get back in'.

Was Michelle legally or morally responsible for Conrad's death? The question is not an easy one, and raises a fundamental issue in legal and moral philosophy concerning what constitutes 'causing' an action. The question may boil down to this: when Conrad stepped into his toxic truck for good, did he act of his own free will? Did Michelle's texts and her plea to 'get back in' the truck persuade Conrad to make that choice for himself, or did they coerce him? When does persuasion become coercion? In this chapter I present the case that Ms. Carter did not coerce Conrad and did not cause his death.

The question of whether Michelle acted badly and should be morally blamed and punished is distinct from the question of whether she should be legally punished. In chapter 2 I cast doubt on the strength of society's interest in morally punishing her. In this chapter I focus on whether Ms. Carter should be held legally responsible for Conrad's death. We may think Michelle acted badly, but we do not inflict legal punishment on those who act badly unless they have violated a law. Those who lie, break a promise, are ungrateful, or refuse to assist others in need may deserve our disapproval, but unless they also violated a law they do not deserve a fine or jail sentence. Did Ms. Carter break any law?

Framing the legal question

Suicide is not against the law, so Ms. Carter can't be accused of conspiracy to commit a crime. Some states do have laws against encouraging or assisting in a suicide, but not Massachusetts. Those laws are controversial: what if suicide is a relief for someone in great physical or mental pain? Does the individual who helps relieve someone of their pain really act badly? What of the implications for the freedom of speech if we punish someone because of what they say? I address whether there ought to be a law against what Ms. Carter did in chapter 5. But here I focus on whether Ms. Carter broke an existing law.

Because the people of Massachusetts never chose to enact a law prohibiting someone from encouraging or assisting in suicide, prosecutors drew on the common law offense of involuntary manslaughter to indict Michelle. Common law offenses are based not on statutes enacted by a legislator but on a body of case law that is refined by judges over time as prior decisions become precedents for future courts. Applying the law on involuntary manslaughter, as we will soon see, requires judgments about whether there is a duty to intervene, and whether one caused harm through reckless conduct. The law doesn't offer clear guidance in answering the latter question, and deciding that, while not the same as deciding whether Michelle acted badly as a matter of morality, can involve moral judgments. (It is worth noting that without clear guidance, individuals lack advance notice as to whether their actions will be deemed illegal, a point I will return to in chapter 4 when we consider whether punishing Michelle will effectively deter others.)

Involuntary manslaughter, in contrast with homicide or intentional murder, is an unlawful killing without an intention to kill. As an example, suppose you drive while you are intoxicated – which is unlawful – and because the alcohol slows your reflexes, when you swerve to avoid an object in the road you kill two pedestrians. You didn't intend to kill them – you didn't commit murder – but you did kill them unlawfully. There are two paths to involuntary manslaughter in Massachusetts. First, one can kill through an *omission*, or a "wanton or reckless failure to act to alleviate a risk involving a life-threatening condition where there is a duty to take reasonable steps to alleviate the risk." If I am a life guard on duty at a pool, and callously ignore the cries of a drowning swimmer, and the swimmer dies, I may have committed involuntary manslaughter by failing to attempt a rescue. Another path to involuntary manslaughter is through the *commission* of an act, as distinct from the failure to act. Here, involuntary manslaughter consists of "an unlawful homicide unintentionally caused by wanton or reckless conduct" in which there is a high degree of likelihood that substantial harm will result to another.[1] The vehicular homicide in the preceding example is an instance of involuntary manslaughter by commission.

Ms. Carter did not commit manslaughter by omission

One might think that Michelle committed manslaughter by omission by failing to prevent Conrad from killing himself. But according to the law, I commit manslaughter by omission only if I had a *duty* to try to alleviate a risk. In ordinary language we distinguish having a duty from having an obligation. Obligations, normally, are voluntarily undertaken; by making a promise we undertake an obligation to keep it. In contrast, one typically has a duty by occupying an office or position.[2] Lifeguards have a duty to assist swimmers, bar owners have a duty to their patrons, and employers have a duty to employees. Others with duties arising from a position they hold include ship captains, and police officers, who have a duty to those in their custody. More generally, duties can arise from assuming a special relationship – such as being a parent, or land owner. According to a leading case from the state of Washington, *Webstad v. Stortini*, a romantic relationship is not a duty-creating special relationship.[3]

Susan Webstad wanted a commitment from Joseph Stortini, who was married to someone else. He invited her to his home and showed a rented movie about divorced people who remarried happily. Later that evening, after she asked him about their future together, he told her he was unwilling to divorce his wife. Susan, who had made prior suicidal gestures, went to the kitchen and took what she told him were eight to ten pills. Stortini

1 *Commonwealth v. Carter*, 474 Mass. 624 (2016); at pp. 630–1.

2 R.B. Brandt, "The Concepts of Obligation and Duty," *Mind* 73:374–93 (1964); at pp. 388–9. Brandt recognizes there are non-paradigmatic uses of 'obligation' and 'duty' as well.

3 924 P. 2d 940 (1996).

reported that he offered to call 911 but she said no; an hour later she again declined help; and he called 911 only after she fell unconscious. She died the next morning. Webstad's estate claimed that Stortini had a duty to aid because he created a risk by leading her on, knowing her fragile mental state, a duty he failed to fulfill by not obtaining assistance immediately. Though the two were romantically involved, and Stortini had once been her employer, the court ruled that this does not create a special relationship that would impose a duty on Stortini. A special relationship would exist only if one party was "entrusted" with the well-being of the other, which was not the case. Having rejected the claim that Stortini had a specific duty based on a special relationship, the court then noted that in the state of Washington I have no general duty to protect an individual from self-inflicted harm or suicide unless, through my acts or omissions, I deprive them of the command of their faculties or the control of their conduct (924 P. 2d. at 945). Stortini did not. Surely he ought to have come to Susan's aid sooner, but he had no legal duty to do so.

A similar principle was used in *People v. Oliver*, with the opposite outcome because the facts differed. The defendant took a drunk man to her house and provided a spoon so he could inject heroin. She then returned to her job, leaving him at the house. When he became unconscious, instead of summoning aid she told her daughter, who was at home, to drag him behind the house, where he'd be out of sight of the neighbors. He died, and she was held responsible. The court ruled that she had a duty to assist because she took charge of him, putting him in a position of helplessness.[4] The trial judge in the Carter case was apparently convinced that Ms. Carter's case is similar, for he found that Ms. Carter had a self-created duty to aid once she told Conrad to get into the truck, knowing it was a toxic environment. But Ms. Carter did nothing comparable to what Oliver did. The toxic environment in the truck was created not by her but by Conrad, when he rigged a water pump to release carbon monoxide. She did not hide Conrad or 'take charge' of him such that he could not be aided by others. That part of the trial judge's decision has been criticized even by those who still think Michelle was guilty of involuntary manslaughter but who think that the basis for her guilt was her commission of a reckless act, not a failure to do her duty.[5]

While Ms. Carter had no legal duty to intervene to prevent Conrad's suicide, morally she may have had a duty of friendship to do so – though she might have thought she was fulfilling that duty by helping Conrad to end his suffering and be 'happy in heaven'. But even if Ms. Carter did act badly

4 210 Cal App 3d 138 (1989).

5 Note, "Commonwealth v. Carter," *Harvard Law Review* 131:918–25 (2018).

in failing to intervene and get Conrad help, that does not justify finding her guilty of breaking the law and putting her in prison – the legal precedents have not established friendship as generating a legal duty to alleviate risks, and she was not entrusted with Conrad's care.

Ms. Carter did not commit manslaughter by commission

The prosecutor argued that Michelle committed manslaughter by commission: that regardless of whether she had a duty to intervene, her encouragement and advice – especially her telling Conrad to 'get back in' the truck – constituted wanton and reckless conduct that caused his death. Ms. Carter's defense attorney responded that words can never overcome a person's will to live. The Massachusetts Supreme Court agreed with the prosecutor. But the issue needs further exploration that includes analysis of what it means to cause something.

Was her conduct reckless?

Before turning to that analysis, I pause briefly over the requirement for involuntary manslaughter by commission that one's conduct be wanton or reckless. One might argue that Michelle's texts or what she said over the phone do not constitute conduct at all, because speech is not conduct. The Supreme Court has distinguished the two in holding that the First Amendment protects only speech;[6] though it has also recognized that some conduct can be regarded as expressive – as 'symbolic speech' – and deserves First Amendment protection.[7] I will turn to this distinction later and for now will just assume that texting words of encouragement or advice can constitute conduct. Here I address whether that conduct was wanton or reckless.

In the law, wanton means an utter disregard for the consequences of one's behavior; reckless can mean much the same thing but also that one foresees the possible consequences but takes the risk nevertheless. Michelle did not disregard the consequences of urging Conrad to get back in the truck: she and Conrad had discussed for weeks the effectiveness of CO poisoning and other methods of suicide and knew what the result of a successful attempt would mean. We might think she still acted recklessly by foreseeing that Conrad would die but taking that risk nevertheless. But to say she 'took

6 *U.S. v. O'Brien*, 391 U.S. 367 (1969) (upholding conviction for burning a draft card, which is conduct).

7 *Texas v. Johnson*, 491 U.S. 397 (1989) (reversing conviction for flag burning, which is protected symbolic speech).

the risk' ignores how she thought it was in Conrad's best interest to end his life – in her mind there was no risk of a horrible result, only a hope that his suffering would be relieved. In *State v. Tentoni*, discussed in chapter 2, Tentoni told Wilson how to obtain and use a fentanyl patch, and Wilson died as a result of following these instructions.[8] Tentoni was convicted of 2nd-degree reckless homicide because Wilson had no desire to die and Tentoni disregarded the unwanted risk his advice created. In contrast, Conrad had expressed a desire to die and had attempted suicide before, and Michelle appears to have believed he would be better off by ending his suffering. To decide whether Michelle's conduct is objectively reckless we will have to wait until chapter 5, where I address the controversial question of whether suicide is necessarily wrong.

Causation

The key requirement of involuntary manslaughter by commission is that one's conduct must have 'caused' the unlawful homicide. I now present the case that Ms. Carter did not cause Conrad's death. Causation is an enormously complex concept, and as I cannot address all its complexities I will focus on some widely known conceptions that were drawn on by the Massachusetts courts deciding Ms. Carter's case.

But for cause

We might identify an earlier event as a cause of a later event if, but for the earlier event, the later event would not have occurred. The earlier event is called a 'but for' cause. Ms. Carter may have been a but for cause of Conrad's dying on or about July 13 in the parking lot of a K-Mart; but in addition to the fact that we can't know this for sure, but for causes are not necessarily the relevant level of causation for determining criminal responsibility.

The prosecutor and a unanimous Massachusetts Supreme Judicial Court were convinced that there was probable cause to believe that "but for [Ms. Carter']s admonishments, pressure, and instructions, the victim would not have gotten back into the truck and poisoned himself to death."[9] But the court did not explain how it could know this was probable. Such counterfactuals are speculative. This is not to say we can never know if something is a but for cause – of course we can. My flipping a switch to 'on' is a but for

8 *State v. Tentoni*, 365 Wis. 2d 211 (2015).

9 474 Mass. 624, 636 (2016). Cf. *Commonwealth v. Carter*, 481 Mass. 352, 363 (2019).

cause of a light going on. But when the event we try to explain involves not behavior that complies with known physical laws, but human action that is a product of will, it is much harder if not impossible to know.[10] We *can* know that stimulating certain neurons is a but for cause of a finger moving, by repeated testing and by tracing the causal mechanism of finger motion. For a complex action such as killing oneself, though, we can't do such testing, and we do not know all the causal mechanisms.

In chapter 1 I discussed the possibility raised by a defense attorney that after Michelle told Conrad to get back into a toxic environment, he may not have. Perhaps he opened the windows, shut off the water pump, and drove around to think, only later poisoning himself. But even if Conrad did get right back into the toxic truck and died 20 minutes later, and even if we somehow knew that Conrad would not have gotten back into his truck if Michelle had not said 'get back in', so that she *was* a but for cause, this does not establish that she is morally or legally responsible for Conrad's death. The google employees who created a search engine algorithm that enabled Conrad to find out how to rig his truck to release carbon monoxide arguably were as much of a but for cause of his death as Michelle, but no one has seriously suggested that Google is responsible for the actions people take after they use its search engine.

There might be countless but for causes of a single event. But for Conrad's parents giving birth to him, or Conrad becoming depressed before he met Michelle, or Ms. Carter's family deciding to vacation in Florida where Michelle could meet Conrad, and numerous other events that led to Michelle and Conrad getting to know each other, Conrad might never have killed himself in precisely the way he did.

In deciding which cause is most relevant for attributing moral and legal responsibility for a consequence, we need to look to a different level of causality that is more proximate. Something is a 'proximate cause' of a suicide if it produces the suicide in the "natural and continuous sequence of events, without which the death would not have occurred."[11] None of the but for causes in the previous paragraph are proximate causes; for example, it is not the natural consequence of Conrad's parents giving birth to him that Conrad would kill himself 18 years later. Did Michelle's encouraging Conrad through her texts, and telling him to 'get back in' the truck, naturally lead Conrad to follow her advice and die as a result?

10 Cf. Hannah Arendt, *The Human Condition* (Chicago: University of Chicago Press, 1958), on the distinction between action and behavior.

11 *Commonwealth v. Rosado*, 434 Mass. 197, 202 (2001).

Proximate cause

One might wonder how Michelle could be a proximate cause of Conrad's death if she was miles away. But a proximate cause needn't be physically close to the event it causes. Conversing through texts can be almost functionally equivalent to conversing face to face. Conversing involves being able to see a reaction and respond to it. Whereas one can't truly converse by exchanging letters because of the time lag between sending a letter and receiving a response, with texts the response can be immediate. To be sure, texting isn't an exact equivalent to face to face interactions, for at least a few reasons. First, when texting one can't see the other party's physical reactions. While texters can insert emoticons, they don't convey nearly the variety and subtlety of physical reactions one can make face to face. Second, there can be substantial gaps between texts. Sometimes Michelle or Conrad wouldn't respond for hours, perhaps because they fell asleep or were busy doing other things. Sometimes Michelle was engaged in multiple texting conversations at the same time. Even so, because texts allow the give and take of conversations, they may present opportunities for moving another to action that merely exchanging letters does not. Justice Cordy, in his opinion for the Massachusetts Supreme Judicial Court, wrote: "Although not physically present when the victim committed suicide, the constant communication with him by text message and by telephone leading up to and during the suicide made the defendant's presence at least virtual."[12] I agree. Someone who persuades another to commit a wrongful act through texts or words spoken on the phone might be as much of a proximate or immediate cause of the wrong as if they had physically been present.

But while someone at a distance can be a proximate cause, whether they actually were is a complicated, fact-dependent question. My approach in answering this question begins by comparing what Ms. Carter did in connection with Conrad's death with what was done in other cases in which the defendant was convincingly found to have caused another to die or commit suicide.

In a Massachusetts case, *Commonwealth v. Catalina*, the defendant supplied heroin to the victim, knowing that she was at risk of abusing it, and the victim died after injecting herself with the heroin. The court found the defendant criminally responsible.[13] In a New York case, *People v Duffy*, the defendant was aware of the suicidal state of the victim when they met; he gave the victim a rifle and ammunition, and goaded him to jump off a porch

12 474 Mass. 624, n. 13.
13 407 Mass 779 (1990).

and to put the gun in his mouth, because he was sick and tired of hearing the victim complain about his life. The victim, who was intoxicated and depressed, then killed himself.[14] The court found that the defendant was a sufficiently direct cause of the suicide to be legally responsible.

Finally, in *Stephenson v. State*, an Indiana case from 1932, the defendant David Stephenson had forcibly restrained, beat, and raped a woman, Madge Oberholtzer, who then ingested poison and died several weeks later. The court held that the defendant was the proximate cause of the suicide even though Ms. Oberholtzer poisoned herself, because she was said not to be of sound mind when she took the poison. Her taking the poison was therefore not a voluntary act. According to the voluntary intervention principle that I discuss in the next section, this leaves the defendant's actions as the most proximate legally relevant cause of her death. The dissent did not think Stephenson caused the victim's death, perhaps because they did not regard suicide as the natural and continuous sequence of events following a rape – though surely they would agree that Stephenson should be convicted for the serious crimes he did commit.[15] But even if we agree with the Stephenson majority, what Ms. Carter did comes nowhere close to what Stephenson did, or Catalina or Duffy.

The prosecutors in the Carter case claimed that by counseling Conrad and alleviating his concerns about killing himself, Ms. Carter assisted in his suicide. But the prosecutors conflate assisting with advising and encouraging. Catalina and Duffy both assisted, Catalina by providing heroin, Duffy by providing a gun and ammunition. Another example of assisting is presented in *Persampieri v. Commonwealth*. Persampieri encouraged his wife to kill herself, and he provided advice when after she placed a rifle between her outstretched legs he told her to take off her shoes so she could reach the trigger; but he went beyond merely encouraging or giving advice when he helped her load the rifle and handed it to her.[16] Persampieri assisted.

Ms. Carter did not do anything for Conrad analogous to providing a gun and ammunition, or loading a rifle, or providing heroin. Her activity was restricted to texting or uttering words. That in itself does not mean she did not assist. It is possible to assist merely with words. I will argue in the concluding section of this chapter that some speech that enables someone to do something they otherwise could not do – speech that offers unique information not otherwise readily available – might reasonably be regarded

14 185 A.D. 2d 371 (NY App. Div. 1992).

15 205 Ind. 141 (Supreme Court of Indiana, 1932).

16 343 Mass. 19 (1961).

as 'assisting'. But Ms. Carter did not provide unique information that Conrad relied on to do what he otherwise would have been unable to do, and so 'assisting' does not seem to fairly characterize what she did.[17] She would have assisted had she supplied Conrad with the water pump he used to generate carbon monoxide, or helped him set it up in his truck. But she did not: she advised and encouraged.

It is tempting to draw a sharp line between speech and conduct and conclude that as Ms. Carter's activity consisted only in speech, she did not meet the threshold requirement to be guilty of involuntary manslaughter of having engaged in 'conduct', and that as speech and not conduct, her activity is protected by the First Amendment. But we should resist drawing the line between speech and conduct so sharply. The Supreme Court has recognized that some speech blurs with conduct and loses the protection of the First Amendment, such as 'fighting words', or speech integral to criminal conduct.[18] There are other instances in which the line between speech and conduct blurs. There are, for example, 'performatives', where by saying certain words one performs an action. Saying 'I do' at a wedding constitutes the act of getting married; saying 'I promise' makes the promise; saying 'I plead not guilty' makes the plea; saying 'I order you to. . .' is the act of commanding.[19] Michelle's words were not performatives. As she had no position of authority over Conrad, they were not an order or command. But she did provide advice and encouragement, and advising and encouraging, while speech, might also be regarded as conduct. So we should not conclude that Michelle fails to meet the threshold 'conduct' requirement for involuntary manslaughter, or that she is automatically protected by the First Amendment. In deciding whether she committed involuntary manslaughter we need to decide not whether her actions were either conduct or speech – a dichotomy that is not clear-cut – but whether one who encourages or advises is the legally relevant cause of what their audience does. Deciding that may resolve the First Amendment issue as well: for if Michelle's speech was the legally relevant cause of Conrad's death it may have been integral to criminal conduct and no longer shielded by the

17 A contrary position was taken in *State v. Melchert-Dinkel*, 844 N.W. 2d 13, 23 (Supreme Ct of Minnesota 2014), holding that providing directed instructions on suicide, even to strangers, and even though the 'instructions' were readily available elsewhere, can be considered assisting.

18 *Chaplinsky v. New Hampshire*, 315 U.S. 568 (1942) (fighting words); *Giboney v. Empire Storage and Ice Company*, 336 U.S. 490 (1949), discussed in chapter 1; and Eugene Volock, "The Speech Integral to Criminal Conduct," *Cornell Law Review* 101(4):981–1052 (2016).

19 See J.L. Austin, *How to Do Things with Words* (Cambridge, MA: Harvard University Press, 1962).

First Amendment. To decide whether Michelle's encouragement or advice caused Conrad to take his own life, we first need to return to Ms. Carter's texts.

Ms. Carter repeatedly gives advice and provides information to Conrad that might help him succeed in killing himself:

7/3/14, 8:51pm:

MICHELLE: I think you should have a back up if the bag doesn't work [referring to Conrad suffocating himself with a plastic bag]

7/4/14, 5:54pm:

MICHELLE: Plastic bag over your head is only a 23% chance of dying. And the overdose on pills and drugs can take up to 2 hours so idk if that's worth it. You want something quick. Gunshots to the head is a 99% chance of working, carbon monoxide is a 80% chance of working. And pills hardly ever work. Carbon monoxide poisoning is the best option . . . Takes up to 15 mins. And there's no pain.

7/4/14, 11:14pm:

MICHELLE: the only way [suffocating yourself with a plastic bag] will work is if you duct tape it to you and tie your hands up or something. And if you really want it, like bad enough to fight your struggle. Otherwise you'll fail.

7/5/14, 4:13pm:

MICHELLE: Do you have heroin? You can overdose on that and drink a lot of alcohol. That's how Cory Monteith died.

7/5/14, 8:03pm:

[Conrad is thinking about using melatonin. Michelle looks that up and texts the following.]

MICHELLE: I don't think that sleeping pill will work because it's a 'safe' pill . . . There isn't really harm in overdosing on it . . . GET BENADRYL! THAT MAKES YOU FALL ASLEEP FAST . . . Get BENADRYL and TYLENOL. . ., just take more than 75,000 [mg of Tylenol] and you'll be good . . . you have to fight to keep the bag on and try your best not to vomit. Its all up to you

7/6/14, 12:08am:

MICHELLE: I'm not telling you to do anything. Its up to you to tell yourself to do it. But yeah, if you take like 4 benedryls, you'll fall asleep in like 15–20 mins. So I'd take those, wait like 10 mins, then take all the Tylenol. . .

CONRAD: first I'm gonna load up on all the sleeping pills I have, wait 30 minutes and then take all the Tylenol. . .

MICHELLE: No don't wait 30 mins! You'll fall asleep before you even take the Tylenol. . .

CONRAD: I'm gonna vomit no matter what I already have a trash bag

MICHELLE: Well you have to try not to . . . I mean you should fall asleep before you can

CONRAD: true

7/6/14, 5:08pm:

[Michelle and Conrad discuss his using carbon monoxide.]

CONRAD: I'm really pushing this one hard Michelle. Like I'm actually happy with the thought it could work.

MICHELLE: Yeah it will work, if you emit 3200ppm of it for 5 to 10 mins, you'll die within a half hour . . . You can also just take a hose and run that from the exhaust pipe

CONRAD: Yes that's what I was thinking . . . my truck is diesel. It's loud and it might not emit CO

MICHELLE: Well that sucks

CONRAD: www.jerryhunt.org/kill.htm. Read this

[The website is entitled 'How to Kill Yourself Using the Inhalation of Carbon Monoxide Gas'.]

7/10/14, 9:50am:

CONRAD: [the generator] stopped working I'm trying to figure out what's wrong with it

2:01pm:

CONRAD: maybe you could help me get it to work

5:04pm:

MICHELLE: Just Google 'how to fix a portable generator' and a lot of stuff comes up I checked . . . OMG GO TO SEARS! THEY SELL THEM THEY CAN HELP . . . they sell a brand new one for 135

[It turns out there was another generator at Conrad's father's house; see 7/10/14, 6:42pm.]

7/12/14, 9:30am:

MICHELLE: Go in your truck and drive in a sparkling lot somewhere, to a park or something

4:28pm:

CONRAD: where??

MICHELLE: a parking lot. . .

CONRAD: so should I keep [the CO] in the back seat? Or front?

MICHELLE: In front. You could write on a piece of paper and tape it on saying 'carbon monoxide' or something if you're scared [that those who find him might be harmed by the gas]

[In fact the water pump generating the CO was found in the back seat of Conrad's truck.][20]

Beginning in early July, Michelle provides advice and information about how to commit suicide: if you use a plastic bag, tie your hands so you can't remove the bag; use Benadryl instead of melatonin; run a hose from the exhaust pipe; put the generator in the front seat; drive to a parking lot. Does this make her a proximate cause of Conrad's death? There are several reasons to think it does not. For one, Conrad often rejects her advice. Moreover, the information Michelle provided was readily available from many sources, and the exchange of information went both ways: Conrad is the one who sent Michelle a link to a website with instructions on how to die using CO poisoning, for example. The contrast with *Tentoni* is again significant. There, Wilson followed Tentoni's specific advice about acquiring and using the fentanyl patch that killed him, and there is no indication he had alternate sources of information he may have relied upon.

One key case in which a court allowed a suit to proceed against a party for what someone else did with the information it made available concerned a civil action of wrongful death, as opposed to a criminal action, and can be distinguished from the Carter case in other ways as well. *Rice v. The Paladin Enterprises, Inc.* concerned a book entitled *Hit Man*, which encouraged the lifestyle of the hit man and gave detailed instructions on how to commit murder.[21] The book's publisher was sued when one of the book's readers followed its instructions and murdered relatives of the plaintiffs. Paladin wanted to establish that the First Amendment provides blanket protection to publishers no matter what effects their books have on people's behavior, and so rather than deny that its book was a proximate cause of the murders, it stipulated, as part of its legal strategy, that it intended to provide would-be criminals with instructions on how to murder and that its book assisted in the murder of the plaintiffs' relatives. Paladin Enterprises lost. Its insurance company paid the plaintiffs several million dollars, and it agreed to cease

20 Michelle Williams, "Michelle Carter Trial: In Days Before Conrad Roy's Death, Teens Shared Suicidal Plan, Selfies," www.masslive.com (June 9, 2017). http://s.masslive.com/2Dq8NLN.

21 238 F. 3d 233 (4th Cir. 1997).

publishing the book.[22] However, the ruling did not address whether in a criminal indictment the publisher would have been responsible for causing the deaths. In any case, the book publisher's role in the murders can be distinguished from Michelle's role in Conrad's suicide. The specific advice Conrad took in poisoning himself with carbon monoxide came from other sources: Michelle merely suggested that Conrad google for information – something Conrad was already aware he could do. Not Michelle but the publisher of the instructions and perhaps Google's search engine were a more proximate cause of his rigging a water pump in his truck.

There may be a narrowly defined category of advice that is so dangerous it should be restricted. We might, for example, think that we should prohibit people from publishing instructions on how to release a highly contagious and fatal virus. But if we did establish a list of such prohibited speech, what Michelle said in her texts would not belong on it. Michelle's texts are distinguishable from *Hit Man. Hit Man* teaches how to murder and provides information not readily available elsewhere. Michelle did not give advice on how to do anything that is illegal, and Conrad could have found this information from many other easily accessible sources himself, and sometimes did.

There would be troubling consequences for the freedom of speech if my giving advice or providing information that helps you commit a wrong would make me criminally responsible for the wrong. The chilling effects on the First Amendment right to the freedom of speech if we hold the author of a webpage or a search engine algorithm responsible for the actions people take based on the information they provide is potentially staggering. In a sense our answer to the question of whether my speech caused you to commit a crime should not depend on these consequences: either it was or it was not the cause. But deciding whether it is a legally relevant cause is a different matter. As Joel Feinberg has noted, there are many causes of an event. For example, in the *Stephenson* case the 'scientific' cause of Ms. Oberholtzer's death was the poison she ingested. But in deciding who is legally to blame for her death the scientific cause is not the only relevant one: we want to know how it came about that she ingested the poison. Feinberg argues that of all the many causes of an event, we "select out one and only one" as more important, based on our "prior assumptions, understandings, and purposes."[23] For the purpose of deciding whether to hold Michelle

22 Calvin Reid, "Paladin Press Pays Millions to Settle 'Hit Man' Case," *Publisher's Weekly*, 245(22) (May 31, 1999).

23 Joel Feinberg, "Causing Voluntary Actions," in Capitan and Merrill, eds., *Metaphysics and Explanation* (Pittsburgh: University of Pittsburgh Press, 1965), p. 36. Cf. Arthur Leavens, "A Causation Approach to Criminal Omissions," *California Law Review* 76(547) (1988).

legally responsible and punish her for Conrad's death, we may want to take into account the consequences to free speech of doing so, as well as other considerations. I would not go so far as some defenders of free speech who invoke the 'slippery slope argument' to oppose virtually all restrictions on speech. They argue that once we restrict some speech for what we think are good reasons, we open the floodgates for censorship. Instead, I think we can say that some advice that is knowingly false and manipulative violates the targeted recipient's autonomy and should be restricted – a point I will return to in the final section of this chapter and in chapter 5. But Michelle's speech doesn't meet those criteria.

Leaving aside the consequences of holding speakers responsible for what others do with their advice, there is a reason why providing advice or information about how to kill oneself can't be the most proximate cause of someone's death. When someone gives advice that results in the recipient doing what the advice recommends, there is an intervening cause that is more proximate: the decision to take the advice.[24]

The voluntary intervention principle

According to the voluntary intervention principle, a proximate cause is canceled if following it there is an intervening voluntary cause. Suppose a bus driver negligently lets you off at the wrong stop in a high-crime area, and you are murdered. The murderer causes your death, not the bus driver. The bus driver's negligence was a but for and even a proximate cause of your death, but that cause is canceled by a more proximate cause – the actions of the murderer.[25] Suppose instead that the negligent bus driver let you off not in a high crime area, but in a location surrounded by pockets of quicksand, and as you got off the bus and walked around to get your bearings you fell into the quicksand and died. According to the voluntary intervention principle the bus driver now *is* the most proximate cause of your death as there was no intervening voluntary cause. Even if Michelle's

24 I distinguish advice from an advisory inducement, e.g., if you do x, I am sure to do y, which can be a veiled threat. See Kent Greenawalt, *Speech, Crimes, and the Uses of Language* (New York: Oxford University Press, 1989), pp. 67–8. My action in response to such 'advice' may be not voluntary but coerced, which, as I discuss shortly, alters our conclusion about causation.

25 The example is from Joel Feinberg, *Harm to Others* (New York: Oxford University Press, 1984), p. 122; for a defense of this principle see H.L.A. Hart and A.M. Honore, *Causation in the Law* (Oxford: Oxford University Press, 1967), 292ff; for criticism see Christopher Pulman, "Voluntary Interventions," in Pulman, ed., *Hart on Responsibility* (London: Springer, 2014).

advice to Conrad – 'get back in' – was a proximate cause of his dying, if he voluntarily chose to get back into the truck he was the intervening voluntary cause of his own death and Michelle would not be responsible. As I will address in the next two sections, this result might change if Michelle could be said to have caused Conrad's voluntary act, or if she coerced Conrad.

Encouraging and inciting vs. advising

So far I have discussed speech that provides advice or information. When someone acts on that advice there is an intervening voluntary cause of their action: their decision to follow the advice. There are other forms of speech that encourage or induce others to cause harm, and there may be more compelling reasons to regulate such speech. Encouraging someone, or inciting them – a form of encouragement that aims to move another to imminent action – is different than merely providing information or advice, because it aims to affect a person's will. Justice Holmes famously argued that someone who maliciously and falsely shouts 'Fire' in a crowded theater does not deserve the shield of the First Amendment.[26] That person doesn't merely provide (false) information but, by shouting, instigates action by creating panic that will foreseeably result in people fleeing in a mad rush to escape a nonexistent threat. If I'm stomped on as a result, we may well say that the responsible cause of my injuries are not the people who ran over me, but is the person who prompted them to run by shouting 'Fire'.

John Stuart Mill, an ardent defender of free speech, recognized that some speech amounts to harmful conduct. Even Mill was willing to say that opinions lose their immunity from regulation when they positively instigate a 'mischievous act'. Mill argues in *On Liberty* that an opinion that corn dealers are starvers of the poor must be allowed when expressed in a newspaper editorial but may justly incur punishment when delivered orally to an excited mob situated in front of a corn dealer's house.[27] Mill does not explicitly say the speaker should be legally punished, only that such acts "may be controlled by the unvariable sentiments, and, when needful, by the active interference of mankind." Still, Mill's position is that speech that incites violent, criminal action likely to cause harm can be subject to some sort of social or state coercion. That view is congruent with the First Amendment doctrine that speech integral to criminal

26 *Schenck v. U.S.*, 249 U.S. 47, 52 (1919).

27 J.S. Mill, "On Liberty," *Collected Works of J.S. Mill* (Toronto: University of Toronto Press, 1977), vol. 18, p. 260 (ch. 3, Par. 1).

conduct is not protected. Are Michelle's words of encouragement like those of the inciter of Mill's excited mob?

Before we answer this, we should look more closely at what she said. The following text exchanges started about a week prior to Conrad's death and indicate how Michelle not only gave advice but encouraged Conrad to go through with the suicide, though she also sometimes expressed concern that he would actually heed her words, and at one point insisted he make the decision for himself.

7/4/14, 12:50pm:

CONRAD: I'm gonna be miserable for the rest of my life. I guarantee you.

MICHELLE: Then you can't fail and you just have to do it. You can't push it off and be afraid anymore. You know once you do it you'll be happy and free in a better place, flying high in heaven.

7/5/14, 7:41pm:

MICHELLE: The sooner you do it the sooner you'll be happy in heaven. You gotta be strong and tough it out and remind yourself that the pain is temporary [referring to overdosing on Tylenol] and it will subside. Its just a few hours and then you'll be pain free forever

7/6/14, 12:08am:

MICHELLE: I'm not telling you to do anything. Its up to you to tell yourself to do it. . .

1:21am:

MICHELLE: If you don't wanna do this, don't do it! I just know you'll always be thinking about it and you're just gonna get worse if you don't get help. . .

1:28am:

MICHELLE: You can't be afraid of something that will make you happy

7/8/14, 5:30pm:

MICHELLE: There's no way you can fail [referring to using CO]

7/9/14:

CONRAD: [after I do it] I'll be happy again

MICHELLE: Yes you will ☺

7/9/14, 6:53pm:

MICHELLE: Do you have the generator?

CONRAD: not yet lol

MICHELLE: WELL WHEN ARE YOU GETTING IT

CONRAD: now

MICHELLE: Okay . . . You better not be bull shiting me and saying you're gonna do this and then purposely get caught

10:45pm:

[Conrad is preparing to start the generator.]

MICHELLE: Wait so this is serious right like the thing is on and you're gonna die soon?

11:02pm:

MICHELLE: Conrad.

11:06pm:

MICHELLE: Conrad please answer me.

7/10/14, 5:32am:

MICHELLE: Conrad.

8:41am:

MICHELLE: Conrad please answer me right now you're scaring me.

9:50am:

CONRAD: I'm ok. . .

7/11/14, 6:23pm:

CONRAD: I'm scared babe

MICHELLE: You called me babe ☺

CONRAD: I'm serious

MICHELLE: Sorry I liked that. But don't be scared. You already made this decision and if you don't do it tonight, you're gonna be thinking about all the time and stuff for the rest of your life and be miserable. You're finally gonna be happy in heaven. No more pain, no more bad thoughts and worries. Youll be free . . . I know how bad u want this and how bad u wanna be happy

7/12/14, 4:28am:

MICHELLE: . . . You're just making it harder on yourself by pushing it off, you just have to do it. . .

9:52am:

MICHELLE: You just need to do it Conrad. The more you push it off, the more it will eat at you.

10:00am:

MICHELLE: If you want it as bad as you say you do, it's time to do it today.

10:21am:

MICHELLE: you just need to do it! You can't keep living this way. You just need to do it like you did last time and not think about it and just do it babe. You can't keep doing this everyday.

10:28am:

MICHELLE: You just need to do it Conrad or I'm gonna get you help. You can't keep doing this everyday. . .

12:57pm:

CONRAD: I'm in the worst pain right now. Like it's unbearable

MICHELLE: I think it's time to do it now then.

MICHELLE: Do you agree. Conrad

3:47pm:

MICHELLE: When you get back from the beach, you gotta d do it. You're ready, you're determined. It's the best time

4:25pm:

CONRAD: Okay I will. . .

6:20pm:

MICHELLE: Okay You can do this.

CONRAD: okay I'm almost there

6:28pm:

MICHELLE: Okay

Michelle encourages Conrad with persistence: 'you just have to do it'; you'll be 'happy' and 'free'; 'the pain is temporary'; there's 'no way the CO will fail'; 'you can't keep living this everyday'. She is the most persistent on July 12, not long before Conrad was found dead, but also the day Conrad says his pain is unbearable.

When Michelle gives advice or provides information, she means to help Conrad achieve a goal that Conrad himself sets. Assisting does this as well – as when Persampieri loaded a rifle so his wife could kill herself. In contrast to giving advice or assisting, encouraging is a form of persuasion, aiming to influence one's will.

Encouraging someone can be distinguished from other techniques for causing others to act. Joel Feinberg notes that if I physically control your movement, or administer behavior modifying drugs to you, or hypnotize or otherwise coerce you, I manipulate you – I cause you to do something, but I don't cause a voluntary act on your part because you never exercise your will.[28] In these cases, I cause what you do and you are not an intervening voluntary cause. When I encourage or persuade you, in contrast, while I may be a but for cause of what results, that result may be more proximately caused by your intervening voluntary act. But there is a gray area of cases where you freely act but I give you a motive, incentive, or reasons to act, influencing your will, and can be said to cause your voluntary action. In some of these cases I *should* be judged a morally relevant cause of what results.

How do we determine whether an instance of encouraging or persuading is the morally relevant cause of another's voluntary act? Feinberg suggests that if you are predisposed to act, I might cause you to act by triggering those predispositions, pushing the right button, so to speak. If you were so strongly predisposed that it took only a slight inducement that could have been created in many ways, your predisposition, not my providing the slight inducement, is the most relevant cause of your voluntary action. But if you were weakly predisposed, and over time I instigated you and substantially fanned your predispositions, making it easier for anyone to pull your trigger, or I pulled hard on your trigger, I would be the more relevant cause of your eventual action.[29] For example, the woman who poisoned herself after Stephenson beat and raped her was probably not predisposed to suicide before she encountered him. Even if her taking the poison was a voluntary act, when Stephenson violated her and took away her dignity he caused her voluntary act. If we viewed just the texts Michelle sent starting in early July, it might look like Michelle steeled Conrad's suicidal predisposition or pulled hard on his trigger, which would shift responsibility for his suicide more to her; but when we step back and look at their previous exchanges, and Conrad's prior history, we see that his predisposition to suicide was firmly in place. Assuming Conrad acted voluntarily and was not coerced – an assumption I defend in the next section – Michelle did not cause his voluntary act. But before turning to the coercion argument, I consider other reasons for not concluding that Michelle's encouragement was a legally relevant cause of Conrad's death.

Recall Feinberg's point that there are many causes of an event and the one we select depends on what our purposes are. (We should keep this point in mind: as I noted earlier, determining whether one is guilty of involuntary manslaughter requires a judgment about causation that may involve the

28 Feinberg, "Causing Voluntary Actions," p. 35.
29 Cf. Feinberg, "Causing Voluntary Actions," p. 35.

weighing of many factors without clear guidance from lawmakers, and this may mean that individuals will lack clear notice of whether their behavior will be regarded as a crime. In chapter 4 I note how this may limit the deterrent benefits of such a law.) If our purpose is to decide whether Michelle should be legally punished, we will want to consider the impact to society of holding certain kinds of persuasion to be punishable offenses. As with the case where Michelle offered information and advice, we need to think about the consequences to the freedom of speech of holding someone to be the legally relevant cause of crimes that their speech persuades others to commit. Consider an author who publishes an elegant and forceful essay about how life is not worth living if it is filled with suffering, an essay that also describes an enticing afterlife of eternal joy. Someone who had been wavering about killing themselves might read the essay whenever they have doubts about going through with an attempt. Suppose that when their pain is as bad as it has ever been, they read and reread key passages of the essay that they had underlined because they were especially moving. Suppose this renews their resolve, and they finally succeed in the suicide attempt. We face the question the *Paladin* court avoided: is the essay's author criminally liable for the death? The consequences of answering yes seem clear: if we hold authors accountable for what they persuade their readers to do, we open the door to widespread self-censorship.

But we should distinguish "public speech" like the essay, which is directed to no one in particular, from "private speech" like Michelle's texts, which is directed to an identifiable individual – though not all speech directed to a particular individual or individuals is private. Justice Cordy had this distinction in mind in permitting the indictment for involuntary manslaughter to stand. He looked to how Michelle's words carried great weight with Conrad. On his view, Michelle had an influence over Conrad that gave her directives a "coercive quality."[30] Words aimed at the public at large would not have that quality.

With this distinction in mind, let's return to Mill's example of the person who incites a mob to attack a corn dealer. Mill says his speech should be protected if it were published as a newspaper editorial – in that case it would be public speech not directed to anyone in particular; but it may warrant punishment if it instead was directed to and incited specific individuals who could foreseeably cause imminent harm.[31] Michelle's speech differs from the inciter's for at least two reasons. First, the mob presumably

30 474 Mass. 624, 634.

31 Foreseeability of causing imminent harm is the key factor that makes otherwise protected speech unprotected in *Brandenburg v. Ohio*, 395 U.S. 444 (1969).

will injure or kill the corn dealer, which is a violent, criminal act; but suicide is not a crime or harm to others. As I will discuss in chapter 4, Mill thinks that the state may punish me only to prevent harm to others, where a harm to others necessarily involves a violation of their rights. Threatening the inciter with punishment might prevent harm to the corn dealer, who has a right not to be attacked violently or killed. But threatening Michelle with punishment would not prevent any violation of Conrad's rights. Conrad has a right not to be coerced, but, I will argue, Michelle did not coerce him. Conrad, like the corn dealer, has a right not to be killed by others, but unlike the corn dealer, Conrad killed himself. Michelle advised, encouraged, and some may want to say incited Conrad; but he has no right not to be spoken to forcefully. Second, Mill's inciter is speaking to a frenzied mob. If they were in such an excited state that they were unable to deliberate, their actions might not be voluntary.[32] In this case, his inciting words are a proximate but for cause, and there is no intervening voluntary intervention to cancel their effect. But, I shall argue in the next section, Conrad acted voluntarily. These differences explain why, on a First Amendment analysis, I do not think Michelle's words would be speech integral to criminal conduct.

Nor am I sure Mill is right if he meant to claim we should legally punish his inciter. The inciter said only that corn dealers starve the poor – he did not then say, 'So kill this corn dealer'. Invoking Feinberg's analysis, if the members of the mob were strongly predisposed to harm the corn dealer – and in his example Mill says they already were excited and situated outside the corn dealer's home – then the inciter may merely have pulled lightly on a trigger that was all set to go off anyway – in contrast with the person who falsely shouts 'Fire' in a theater, causing people to run who were not otherwise going to run. Mill's inciter surely did not coerce the mob. Whether he is responsible depends on to what extent he inflamed them. Michelle's texts of encouragement did not incite Conrad to imminent action. I'm willing to say that her saying 'get back in' may constitute incitement, as long as we don't understand 'inciting' to necessarily mean 'causing'. But while incitement is more problematic than encouragement, it may not be enough to convict her of manslaughter unless it means she caused him to get back in. As Conrad was already strongly predisposed to killing himself, Michelle would have caused this only if she overbore Conrad's will. I now turn to the crucial question of whether Michelle exerted so much pressure on Conrad that he did not act voluntarily when he took his own life.

32 Raphael Cohen-Almagor, "J.S. Mill's Boundaries of Freedom of Expression: A Critique," *Philosophy* 92(4):565–96 (2017); at pp. 587–8.

Coercion

If Michelle influenced Conrad but did not create his predisposition to kill himself or substantially fan it so as to diminish the force needed to trigger it, and Conrad's suicide was his own voluntary act, then his act and not the prior influence is the relevant cause of his death. But if Conrad's act was not free or deliberate – if, as the *Webstad* court would put it, Michelle's "acts or omissions directly or indirectly deprive[d]" Conrad of the command of his faculties or the control of his conduct, Michelle and not Conrad should be regarded as the relevant cause of death, even if this had troubling implications for privacy and free speech.[33] To apply the voluntary intervention principle we must ask whether Michelle coerced Conrad.

Conrad's aunt said on ABC's nationally broadcast *20/20* show that Michelle 'forced' Conrad to kill himself, and that 'but for her actions', he'd still be alive. Justice Cordy and Judge Moniz took the same position. Justice Cordy suggested that "there was evidence that the defendant's actions overbore the victim's willpower."[34] When the case went back to the trial court, Judge Moniz agreed. He focused on Michelle's words 'get back in': in his mind, her saying this caused Conrad to get into the truck, causing his death. Judge Moniz recognizes that Conrad rigged the water pump to release CO in his truck by himself and had a history of depression and even prior suicide attempts. But when Conrad exited the truck to speak with Michelle, according to the judge, he broke the chain of self-causation, and Michelle's instruction then became causative. A recent Note in the *Harvard Law Review* agrees that a guilty verdict was "entirely defensible," on the theory that "a defendant is responsible for the acts of another when his conduct completely overwhelms the victim's free will."[35] Carter's "constant pressuring and definitive command to 'get back in'" overwhelmed Roy such that his act could be attributed to her (923). Remarkably, the author compares what Michelle did to Conrad with what Stephenson did to Ms. Oberholtzer, the woman who took poison after he abducted, beat, and raped her. She was "in the custody and absolute control of the defendant" (924 n. 57) and apparently, to the author, so was Conrad. Of course the cases are entirely different: Stephenson intimidated his victim, had her guarded by his accomplices, forced her to accompany him, and physically assaulted and raped her. As we will soon see, Michelle wanted Conrad to spend more time with her, but he refused – and she had no ability to force the matter. The Note's author characterizes Michelle's interactions with Conrad as a "consistent course of coercive behavior" (925), and says that her guilt stems from that

33 *Webstad v. Stortini*, 924 P. 2d. 940, 945 (1996).

34 474 Mass. 624, 635. Cf. *Commonwealth v. Carter*, 481 Mass. 352 (2019), n. 10.

35 Note, *Harvard Law Review* 131:918–25 (2018); at pp. 918, 921–2.

behavior and not just her words; but the author points to no behavior apart from her words as evidence, and ignores what Michelle said through most of June 2014, during which time she repeatedly tried to dissuade Conrad and get him help.

In presenting the case that Conrad was not coerced, I do not assume that texts from a distance can't coerce: earlier I argued that they are almost functionally equivalent to face to face conversations. Someone with a virtual presence can bear on another's will. Instead, I rely on two reasons for concluding that Michelle did not coerce Conrad: she did nothing remotely like threatening him; and she did not have power over him that would let her control what he did, or 'command' him.

There are at least two paradigmatic ways in which I might overbear your will or coerce you. First, I can threaten you. A classic example is presented in Blake Edwards's 1962 film *Experiment in Terror* in which a man kidnaps a bank teller's younger sister, whom he threatens to kill unless the teller gets him money from the bank. Michelle never threatened Conrad with adverse consequences if he failed to kill himself; when she said 'get back in', no threat was attached. Michelle not only did not threaten Conrad, or limit his options – she never presented him with a choice, except when she texted: "You just need to do it Conrad or I'm gonna get you help" (July 12, 10:28am).

Another paradigmatic case of coercion would be something like hypnosis, where one literally controls another person so that they no longer can act of their own free will. As an example, consider the evil villain Kilgrave in the Marvel series *Jessica Jones*. He uses his power of mind control to make others do deplorable things they would never choose to do, and worse, he makes them unaware of what he made them do. Kilgrave grossly violates an individual's autonomy. Ms. Carter had nothing remotely resembling this power over Conrad. In one text she indicates that she respects Conrad's autonomy, saying "I'm not telling you to do anything and its up to you to tell yourself to do it."

There are some text exchanges suggesting that Conrad was reluctant to kill himself and Michelle pressured him, but they are ambiguous:

7/5/14, 10:45pm:
MICHELLE: . . . If you want it you'll do whatever it takes
CONRAD: I don't think I have it in me
MICHELLE: I knew it
CONRAD: I'm too scared . . . you're right I don't have it in me

11:30pm:
[After they discuss Conrad's taking Tylenol to overdose]

MICHELLE: Are you gonna do it or not?

CONRAD: Yeah. Can you stop rushing me please. Like I'm just thinking. My life is gonna end.

MICHELLE: I'm not rushing you. I'm just asking you because I wanna try to change your mind before it's too late. I just wanna make sure you're 100% sure you wanna do this.

CONRAD: yes I am. I'm just thinking.

Conrad says he doesn't think he can go through with an attempt; and he says he feels that Michelle is rushing him. This might suggest that Michelle's encouragement made all the difference. Michelle is clearly making Conrad uncomfortable, as anyone wavering about a decision might be made to feel when someone emphasizes one of the options they are considering: but is she coercing him? Conrad says "I'm just thinking" twice, indicating he is not putting his fate in Michelle's hands but is weighing choices for himself. Earlier that evening Conrad does text: "I'm putting all my trust in you. I don't trust myself" (7/5/14, 7:53pm). But their later exchanges suggest he didn't literally mean that. Nothing in their texts indicates either that Michelle threatened Conrad or that she could control him.

If anything, the power relationship went the other way. Numerous texts between Michelle and Conrad during the month of June 2014, which have not been mentioned in the press, court cases, or legal commentaries, suggest that Michelle was seeking something more from their relationship, but Conrad resists:

6/19/14, 5:00pm:

MICHELLE: you were the first boy who made me feel loved and important, and visible. And I want more than anything for you to be in my life forever . . . I'll always love you.

CONRAD: I'll always love you too . . . I'm sorry for being an asshole to you all those times. . .

5:51pm:

MICHELLE: you already made it clear you don't wanna date again

CONRAD: when did I say that

6:01pm:

MICHELLE: I've asked you and every time you say no, that it won't work

6:17pm:

MICHELLE: Conrad?

6:34pm:
CONRAD: idk. I don't' remember saying that
MICHELLE: So you'd wanna?
CONRAD: idk. Maybe

8:22pm:
MICHELLE: But yeah we gotta go on dates ☺
CONRAD: If I make it that far

10:53pm:
MICHELLE: We need to go on a date
CONRAD: Or just hanging out can be our date lol

6/21/14:
MICHELLE: I'm scared that when you finally get better, that you're gonna forget about me . . . You won't will you? Because you did that in the past. I was there for you and helped you and all that and then you just like forgot about me.
CONRAD: no I won't

6/22/14, 10:05pm:
[Michelle had wanted to come over to Conrad's, but he didn't reply.]
MICHELLE: Guess I'm not coming over then

6/26/14, 7:06pm:
CONRAD: Do you still love Alice?
MICHELLE: Idk [Michelle explains she is not 'bi' but there was one girl she loved once.]
CONRAD: Well don't anymore. She's gone and you can't have her back.
MICHELLE: I know and its not like we would have been together forever or anything because I have you
CONRAD: Yes I guess
MICHELLE: Guess?
CONRAD: if I can somehow get out of this mess
MICHELLE: You'll get thru it, one day at a time. Do u think we have a future?
CONRAD: a future?? I don't think I have a future at this rate. . .

7:37pm:
CONRAD: We should be like Romeo and Juliet at the end.
MICHELLE: Haha I'd love to be your Juliet. . .

6/27/14, 7:42pm:

CONRAD: I'M THE WORST I'VE EVER BEEN. . .

MICHELLE: Do you wanna come over tomorrow? Please . . . I HAVE THE BEST IDEA OMG YOU NEED TO COME OVER PLEASE . . . Can you?

CONRAD: No I'm busy. . .

6/28/14, 12:42pm:

MICHELLE: You say you want to hangout but then when the time comes you don't want to. . .

1:10pm:

CONRAD: I'll hang out Monday. . .

MICHELLE: Not tonight?

CONRAD: no. sorry

7:52pm:

MICHELLE: Haha love you

CONRAD: I know

MICHELLE: . . .

CONRAD: ???????

MICHELLE: Say you love me

CONRAD: you love me

6/30/14:

MICHELLE: Do you want to ????

CONRAD: want to what

MICHELLE: See fireworks on Friday

CONRAD: I'm gonna be in Falmouth

Conrad is repeatedly evasive about a commitment, and even about seeing Michelle in person. The exchanges tend to cast doubt on Justice Cordy's assessment that Michelle's words carried 'great weight' with Conrad to the point where they had a coercive quality, and on Judge Moniz's assumption that Michelle had power over Conrad and overbore his will.

Justice Cordy and Judge Moniz both focused on one thing above all else: that Michelle told Conrad to 'get back in' the toxic truck; we saw that one commentator interprets these words as a 'command'. We know Conrad was wavering about committing suicide. He had made attempts in the past and researched more effective means. He secured a generator and rigged his truck to release CO. Judge Moniz says none of that matters once he got out of the truck and that Michelle's words must have caused him to get back in. But Michelle was no Kilgrave. Even if those words were shouted at Conrad – which we don't know since we have only Michelle's account of what she said two months later, not a recording of how she said them – there is nothing that we know about their relationship that lets us conclude that Conrad's decision was not ultimately his own. Throughout the month of June Michelle insisted that Conrad get help, but he resisted her pleas. Why think he suddenly was under her spell and she could make him do things he didn't already want to do?

Moreover – and this may be the most important point – we just don't know the context in which Michelle said 'get back in'. Suppose Conrad had said to Michelle, "I really want to do this and the only thing holding me back is not knowing whether you really will be there for my family and explain to them why I did this." Suppose Michelle, who 6 hours earlier received a text from Conrad saying his pain was unbearable, replied, gently: "Yes I will, I will tell them you are happier this way because you were suffering so much: so you can get back in." If that is how the conversation went, would Michelle have overborne Conrad's will?

Conclusion: can words kill?

Can words kill? Consider a terminally ill patient kept alive by a life-support machine that is set up such that to turn it off – and kill the patient – one must press an Off button marked A, which is next to a button marked B that, when pressed, permanently disables the Off button. I, but not the patient, know that the one marked A is the Off button. The patient says to me, "I want to die, so do I press button A or B?" I say "A," and then the patient presses button A and dies. Did my speech kill him? Suppose instead that the patient says to me, "I want to die, but I'd rather not press the button myself"; or the patient is physically unable to press the clearly labeled Off button. So he asks me to, and I do. Here I assist, rather than provide advice or information.

The cases are similar: my words led to the patient's death just as did my pressing the button. Words can cause someone's death. But not all causes are morally relevant. Where I merely tell the patient which button is which, I am a but for cause, but there is an intervening voluntary cause of his death that is more proximate. I am merely helping the patient carry out his will. Where I press the button, I am the most proximate cause of death, though again I am merely enabling the patient to carry out his will.

It is tempting to distinguish the cases by saying that providing information is 'speech', whereas pressing the button is 'assisting', which is 'conduct', and to argue that I may be punished for my conduct but not my speech. But as I argued earlier, these distinctions are problematic. Some speech blurs with conduct. Sometimes when I provide information I assist. Suppose the buttons are labeled in Chinese, which the patient does not understand but I do, and it would be nearly impossible for him to find someone else who can translate Chinese; if I translate the labels and tell the patient which is the Off button, my words may constitute assistance as they enable what the patient could not do left to his own devices. If we are in a jurisdiction in which it is against the law to assist in suicide, I might then be just as culpable as when I pressed the button.[36]

Rather than focus on whether we classify my action as conduct or speech, or as assisting or advising, we should ask whether I respected the patient's autonomy and whether their death resulted from their informed, voluntary decision. One reason we may think that pressing the button *is* more problematic is that if I press the button there is a chance that the patient changes his mind but is unable to express this to me in time. The principle that we should respect an individual's autonomy and ensure that his decision is informed and voluntary accounts for why my moral responsibility changes dramatically if the information I provide to the patient is knowingly false. If I know the patient will recover but I lie and tell him he never will, I undermine the patient's autonomy: if he presses the button as a result, in a sense he does so voluntarily, but in a sense he does not, because he would not have chosen to do so had I not lied; his choice was not informed.

Michelle did not assist Conrad in killing himself. She did not enable Conrad to do what he could not otherwise do on his own, or provide false information or information Conrad could not have easily gathered on his own. Michelle may have been a but for cause of Conrad's dying just when he did – though we can't know this for certain. But I have argued that a fact-specific inquiry indicates that Conrad made his own decision without being threatened or controlled by Michelle – his voluntary choice was the most proximate and morally relevant cause of his death.

That the fact-specific inquiry drew on texts intended only for Michelle and Conrad takes me back to the concern about privacy. The only way to counter those who claim that Michelle coerced Conrad is to show that the snippets of texts they rely on do not adequately portray what happened. I did this by consulting even more texts. If we are going to try people in a court of law because their words may have influenced those with whom they have a personal relationship, then reaching a fair conclusion in our fact-specific inquiry – a conclusion that does not rely on snippets taken out

36 Cf. *State v. Melchert-Dinkel*, 844 N.W. 2d 13 (2014): providing directed instructions about hanging oneself can count as 'assisting' – though the information was readily available from many sources.

of context – may force us to uncover still more information, and this has dangerous consequences not only for the freedom of speech but for privacy.

It may seem hypocritical of me to have argued in chapter 2 that Ms. Carter's texts should remain private, and then invade her privacy by calling attention to those texts in all their intimate details. I recognize the irony and have two responses. First, the texts have become a matter of legitimate public concern and are newsworthy. Second, the texts have already been widely published and repeatedly cited – though not all the texts that are important for fairly judging the case have received sufficient attention. As a practical matter, since Michelle's and Conrad's privacy has already been violated, continued discussion of the material no longer frustrates a reasonable expectation of privacy. But further invasions of her privacy would not have been needed had Ms. Carter never been charged.

Michelle and Conrad had a legitimate interest in keeping private their deeply personal interactions. But their legitimate privacy interests can give way if there is a compelling public interest in exposing this information. The primary public interest would be to determine if Ms. Carter was responsible for Conrad's death and, if she was, to punish her. I have challenged the position that she was legally responsible: while she may have influenced Conrad, it was his choice to get back in his truck and ultimately take his own life. Still, there could be a public interest in punishing Michelle. There is an interest in blaming those who act badly. And even if they are not the morally or legally relevant cause of death, there may be an interest in deterring people from encouraging suicide in the future. In the next chapter we consider the strength of the interest in punishing Ms. Carter to see if it outweighs the interest in privacy.

4 Punishment

Overview

Michelle Carter and Conrad Roy wanted to keep their intimate exchanges private. In chapter 2 I argued that individuals can reasonably expect privacy in phone conversations and texts that aren't in plain view or earshot of others, at least when they converse with someone they know and trust. But the legitimate privacy interests they each had might be outweighed by compelling public interests. What public interest might be served by exposing their private conversations?

The public certainly would find the texts interesting, even captivating. Making the texts available would allow the public to be privy to the thoughts and secrets of two burdened teens facing personal crises and life or death choices. But that something is of interest does not mean the public's interest in knowing about it is compelling or even legitimate. The public has a legitimate interest in knowing about newsworthy events, but we should distinguish what is newsworthy from what merely satisfies one's curiosity or is entertaining. The fact that a rape took place is newsworthy, but a video the rapist made of his assault is not; broadcasting it would serve only prurient interests.[1] This is not to say that Michelle and Conrad's conversations were lurid or prurient; and the fact that a teenager died is legitimate news. Because the prosecutor decided to charge Ms. Carter with involuntary manslaughter, her possible role in the suicide became newsworthy. But had the prosecutor not charged Ms. Carter, information conveyed in the thousands of text exchanges between Michelle and Conrad as well as those between Michelle and some of her other friends, such as that Michelle struggled with an eating disorder, was once in love with a girl, or liked the television show *Glee*,

1 *Doe v. Luster*, 2007 Cal.App. Unpub. Lexis 6042 (2007).

would not have been anyone's business other than those Michelle chose to confide in.

The prosecutors believed there were good reasons to indict Ms. Carter. They believed they had probable cause to think she was responsible for Conrad's death, and so they pursued the public interest in punishing criminals. That interest could in theory be served by permitting only the attorneys and judges to see the texts – but in the U.S. such evidence is in the public record. In this chapter I cast doubt on the weight of the public interest in punishing Ms. Carter.

In chapter 3 I argued that Ms. Carter is not legally responsible for Conrad's death and did not commit a punishable offense in the state of Massachusetts. While Ms. Carter would have been guilty of violating a law that prohibited individuals from encouraging another to commit suicide, Massachusetts had no such law. In this and the next chapter I argue that there should be no such law. One might take the position that we should have such a law so that we can express blame for behavior we think is morally wrong or deter conduct that leads to bad consequences. In chapter 5 I will challenge that position by arguing that assisting, advising, or encouraging someone to kill themselves is not necessarily morally wrong and need not lead to bad consequences. In this chapter I address the more general question of whether the fact that society judges an individual's actions to be immoral means that this individual should be legally punished, and whether doing so in Ms. Carter's case would fulfill the purposes for which we have the practice of legal punishment.

I focus on the practice of legal rather than moral punishment. In chapter 2 I discussed the problematic nature of non-legal or moral punishment, which involves morally reproaching or shaming those we think have acted badly. Lacking clearly accepted standards for what counts as acting badly, each person becomes their own judge; the accused receives no due process, which exacerbates the risk that people will be judged unfairly based on snippets taken out of context; and unlike legal punishment, moral punishment is not part of a coordinated response that ensures that the punishment will be measured and proportionate. Given these potential abuses, it is unlikely that society's interest in morally punishing Ms. Carter would be compelling enough to outweigh privacy interests. With legal punishment there are more clearly defined rules for reaching judgments, advocates are highly trained, and judges are scrutinized by courts of appeal, reducing though not eliminating the risk of misjudgment.

I focus on the two leading theories of legal punishment: retributive and utilitarian. The typical retributivist sees the purpose of punishment as upholding justice, affirming that certain actions are wrong, and expressing disapproval of the criminal. The retributivist, generally, sees punishment as 'punitive' – inflicting pain or unpleasantness on the criminal in response to their wrongful conduct. Those who were angered by what they perceived as Ms. Carter's callousness when she told Conrad to 'get back in' a poison-filled truck, and who were furious when she was released pending her appeal, appear to adopt a retributive attitude in wanting to see her suffer as payback. But as we will see, not all retributivists regard punishment as payback for those who act badly; and many retributivists explicitly distinguish retribution from revenge.[2] Whereas revenge is motivated by the subjective feelings of hurt that victims of crime experience, retribution is the upholding of justice, which is objective in as much as it appeals to standards set out in the law and is carried out not by the victim or their loved ones, but by the state.[3]

For the utilitarian, in contrast, the goal of punishment is not to deliver justice, but to increase the overall welfare or happiness in society – to increase 'social utility'. Punishment does this by deterring future crimes, incapacitating dangerous people, and reforming criminals. The utilitarian argues that a society that did not punish criminals would be a very dangerous and unhappy place in which we would live in constant fear of being victimized. Punishment holds potential criminals in check; it promotes our welfare by allowing us to avoid danger and live without this fear.

Sometimes the goals emphasized by these two competing approaches to punishment conflict. For example, a punishment that a retributivist would regard as too harsh for a relatively minor offense might be justified to the utilitarian as an effective and efficient deterrent.[4] Or a retributivist may insist that we punish a criminal because they deserve it, while a utilitarian would prefer to release the criminal if they provide information that enables us to put away their far more dangerous accomplice. But each theory captures essential reasons for punishing.[5] If we are retributivists, punishing Ms. Carter would make sense only if she deserved punishment, and for many retributivists that would be the case only if she culpably wronged Conrad. But the question of whether Michelle is blameworthy or acted badly is not as central to utilitarians. They would focus on whether punishing Ms. Carter would make society better off in the future, perhaps by decreasing the number of people who will be encouraged to commit suicide.

2 For example, Hegel, *Philosophy of Right*, tr. Wood (Cambridge: Cambridge University Press, 1991), Par. 101 and Addition [Hereafter PR].

3 Mark Tunick, *Punishment: Theory and Practice* (Berkeley: University of California Press, 1992), pp. 84–90.

4 Louis Kaplow and Steven Shavell, *Fairness v. Welfare* (Cambridge: Harvard University Press, 2006), ch. 6.

5 See Tunick, *Punishment*, ch. 5.

Retributive purposes of punishment

Kant and Hegel

Perhaps the most striking statement of a retributivist position is this passage by Immanuel Kant from his *Metaphysics of Morals*:

> Even if a civil society were to be dissolved by the consent of all its members (e.g., if a people inhabiting an island decided to separate and disperse throughout the world), the last murderer remaining in prison would first have to be executed, so that each has done to him what his deeds deserve and blood guilt does not cling to the people for not having insisted upon this punishment; for otherwise the people can be regarded as collaborators in this public violation of justice.[6]

Here Kant implies that the reason we punish has nothing to do with the effect punishment would have on future crime rates. We punish because justice demands it. But Kant's position on punishment is complicated, because he distinguishes retributive punishment, which is imposed by someone guided by moral standards, from pragmatic punishment, which is imposed by the state to reform or deter. The same Kant who writes that we must punish the last murderer on death row for the sake of justice also says that "[a]ll punishments imposed by sovereigns and governments are pragmatic. They are designed either to correct or to make an example."[7] By punishing those who violate rights we protect those rights, which for Kant is the very reason we enter into civil society (MM 264, 307–8). Even though Kant says that the point of instituting a practice of legal punishment is to deter people from violating rights, he still adopts a strongly retributivist position that when we punish we must adhere to the requirements of justice. In another famous passage from the *Metaphysics of Morals* Kant opposes a proposal to mitigate the deserved punishment of a person on death row if he participates in dangerous experiments that could yield beneficial results, a proposal that utilitarians may endorse: "A court would reject with contempt such a proposal from a medical

6 Immanuel Kant, *Metaphysics of Morals*, tr. Mary Gregor (Cambridge: Cambridge University Press, 1991), p. 333 [Hereafter MM; page citations are from the Prussian Academy of Sciences edition, included in Gregor's translation].

7 Immanuel Kant, *Lectures on Ethics*, tr. Louis Infield (New York: Harper, 1963), p. 55. [Hereafter LE]. Cf. MM 220. I discuss Kant's distinction between legal and moral punishment in "Is Kant a Retributivist?" *History of Political Thought* 17:60–78 (1996). Cf. Thomas Grey, "Serpents and Doves: A Note on Kantian Legal Theory," *Columbia Law Review* 87:580–91 (1987).

college," Kant writes, "for justice ceases to be justice if it can be bought for any price whatsoever" (MM 332). When we punish the guilty we must give them exactly the punishment they deserve, no more and no less. Kant takes this position in part because he believes that human beings should not be treated merely as a means to some end – a point I return to later. But Kant's objection is also based on a commitment to a principle of just deserts. Although Kant thinks we legally punish to deter wrongdoers or reform them, he insists that a punishment fit the crime, so that each has done to them what their acts deserve.

Most retributivists, though, take the position that the reason we have the practice of legal punishment is not to reduce future crime but to mete out justice and blame wrongdoers.[8] While the fact that punishment may deter crime may be a fortunate result, it is not the reason we punish. The German philosopher Georg Wilhelm Friedrich Hegel argues, for example, that the reason we punish is not to deter or reform but to vindicate right: "To leave crime unpunished would let it be seen as right" and "count as valid"; it would "make crime seem justified."[9] In his *Philosophy of Right*, Hegel identifies various practices and institutions without which we would not be free. Such practices and institutions are 'right', and violating their requirements is a wrong. For example, Hegel argues that private property is essential to our freedom, and so a thief who steals property commits a wrong. If we never punished those who stole property, it would be meaningless to say there is a right to property. One might interpret Hegel's account of why we have the practice of legal punishment to be, like Kant's, forward looking: for Hegel we punish to avoid a future in which crimes no longer are regarded as wrong. But Hegel explicitly rejects the view that we legally punish to deter or reform. While he allows that deterrence and reform theories can influence the precise amount of punishment we inflict, Hegel insists that they do not determine the 'nature' of punishment: "Deterrence and reform are important goals, and one can ask what reforms or security society demands, but another question is what justice or right demands, and every human being feels this difference."[10]

Retributivists such as Kant and Hegel would agree that if an individual were guilty of violating a law, they should be punished. For Hegel, we must punish to vindicate right; for Kant, each must receive what their act deserves, albeit with the goal of deterring future violations of rights. By 'guilty', the

8 Cf. Joel Feinberg, "The Expressive Function of Punishment," *Monist* 49(3):397–423 (1965).

9 PR 99. Quotes are from Hegel, *Vorlesungen über Rechtsphilosophie*, 4 vols., ed. Karl-Heinz Ilting (Stuttgart: Friedrich Fromann, 1973), vol. 3, pp. 310, 662, 549 [Hereafter cited as Rph].

10 Rph vol. 4:286; corresponding to PR 99 Rem.

typical retributivist means not merely that the individual violated a criminal law, but that they were blameworthy. For Hegel, we need to vindicate right only if right has been attacked. Hegel distinguishes 'non-malicious' wrongs, an example of which is that I take your property accidentally, thinking it is mine, from crime, because the non-malicious wrongdoer respects right in general, and simply makes a mistake. For Hegel, we should punish only crimes, not non-malicious wrongs, because the non-malicious wrongdoer has not flouted right and is not blameworthy. Nor should we punish those who are not accountable for their actions because of some incapacity. In this category Hegel includes 'imbeciles', 'lunatics', and 'infants', but not those suffering a temporary incapacity such as "momentary blindness, the excitement of passion, [or] intoxication" (PR Pars. 120, 132 Rem).

If I were hypnotized into robbing a bank, or if I committed a crime when I was insane, or a mere child, I would not be accountable for my actions, and the retributivist would not think I should be punished. But Ms. Carter was not so young, nor was she insane, under hypnosis, or otherwise subject to serious incapacity. Dr. Peter Breggin, the expert witness brought forth by Ms. Carter's defense attorney, tried to argue incapacity by testifying that Ms. Carter was involuntarily intoxicated from her medication – but that turned out to be an unconvincing and misguided strategy. The difficulty in deciding whether the retributivist would think the purposes of punishment would be served by punishing Ms. Carter lies elsewhere than in deciding if she was accountable. Rather, it lies in deciding whether what she did counts as a legally punishable wrong.

Ms. Carter did not clearly violate a law as there was no law in Massachusetts prohibiting someone from encouraging another to commit suicide. The prosecutor resorted to the common law offense of involuntary manslaughter, but to convict her on that charge we must conclude that she caused Conrad to kill himself by coercing him, a conclusion I rejected in chapter 3. When we try to apply Kant's or Hegel's retributive theories to the Carter case it becomes apparent that their theories are ambiguous where the behavior being punished does not clearly violate the law or infringe upon a right, or where our conclusion of whether a criminal law was violated depends on moral judgments we are left to make with little guidance from the law. We might think that even if Ms. Carter did not violate a law that was clearly in place, she acted badly and deserves to be blamed. Ms. Carter, the argument goes, should have gotten Conrad help rather than encourage him to end his life. However, retributivists do not necessarily take the position that we should legally punish individuals who act immorally.

One might have thought the opposite, given that retributivists typically see the central purpose of punishing as the righting of wrongs. But we need to distinguish retributive theory from the distinct position that the law properly is used to punish those who act immorally. The latter view is called legal moralism and is a theory about what actions should be illegal. Retributivism, in contrast, is a theory about why we should inflict punishment on those who break the law. Legal moralists, who take the position that we should legally punish those who act immorally, are likely to be retributivists in thinking that we punish to express blame. But not all retributivists are legal moralists. Not all retributivists would define wrongful conduct as conduct that is immoral. In fact, not all retributivists regard the purpose of punishment as expressing moral disapproval of the criminal: there is a range of retributive positions concerning the connection between law and legal punishment on the one hand, and morality on the other. In presenting this range I begin by turning to a retributivist who entirely disavows the view that punishment should involve a moral judgment that the criminal acted badly.

Mabbott

In his classic 1939 article "Punishment," J.D. Mabbott asks "[u]nder what circumstances is the punishment of some particular person justified and why?"[11] His answer is that we punish solely because a law was broken, and not to achieve some future benefit such as the reduction of crime. Mabbott also takes the position, surprisingly so for a self-proclaimed retributivist, that we do not punish to cast blame. For Mabbott, "a 'criminal' means a man who has broken a law, not a bad man" (154). He sees no essential connection between punishment and moral or social wrongdoing. This lack of connection explains why we don't punish an individual retrospectively for committing a wrong that at the time was not against the law but now is. If the purpose of punishing is to express blame, we have just as much reason to punish them for their wrongdoing whether or not what they did was at the time illegal. But for Mabbott, proper punishment can be inflicted only if a law was broken, and nothing more is necessary (155). The point of punishing is not to judge those who act badly: "For a moral offence, God alone has the *status* necessary to punish the offender" (154). Nor is the essential purpose of punishing to deter. Punishment may have the effect of reforming or deterring, but if it does, that has nothing to do with why we are justified in punishing someone – those effects are just icing on the cake (153).

Mabbott makes a logical or conceptual point that if someone breaks the law we must punish them – that punishment "is a corollary of law-breaking" (160). When he asks why we should have criminal laws in the first place, and what laws there should be, he suggests the answer is given by the principle of utility (161). But he insists that just because we may choose to have

11 J.D. Mabbott, "Punishment," *Mind* 48:152–67 (1939); at p. 152.

laws in order to increase social utility does not mean that the purpose of punishing a particular individual is to deter, reform, or incapacitate. Mabbott would also say that if we chose to have laws in order to blame wrongdoers, that would not mean the purpose of punishing a particular individual is to blame them. His point is that judges and jurors should not decide to punish because of the "moral baseness of the accused," or even because of the need to deter others. The only consideration should be the suspect's legal guilt (167). If we are Mabbott-type retributivists and were convinced by the case presented in chapter 3 that Ms. Carter did not violate a law, we would not punish Ms. Carter; if instead we believed Ms. Carter was guilty of involuntary manslaughter, we would want her punished, but not to express blame or deter others – we would punish only because that is what we must do to law violators.

Legal moralism

Mabbott's theory stands at one end of a continuum of retributive theories, a continuum defined by the connection that is seen between legal punishment and morality. Mabbott denies any such connection. On the other end of the continuum are legal moralists, who see law and punishment as tools to blame people for their immoral acts and to promote virtue. 'Legal moralism' usually refers to a theory about what actions should be illegal. In contrast to liberals who argue that the coercive force of the law should be used only to prevent individuals from harming or offending others, or paternalists who argue that the law may also be used to prevent people from harming themselves, legal moralists argue that law may be used to prevent immoral actions even if those actions do not harm anyone or violate anyone's rights – possible examples being public nudity, sodomy, using marijuana, or using profanity. 'Legal moralism' does not usually refer to a theory of why we legally punish; but it is a helpful term to characterize the view of some retributivists who, in complete opposition to Mabbott, see the essential purpose of punishment as expressing a moral judgment.

Walter Berns is the exemplar. He argues that we punish to express our righteous anger.[12] Showing our anger, on his view, is a morally appropriate way of holding humans responsible for their blameworthy actions and reveals "a profound caring" for them (334–5). It also expresses our commitment to justice: "Punishment arises out of the demand for justice, and justice is demanded by angry, morally indignant men; its purpose is to satisfy that moral indignation" and not just to promote law abidingness (340).

12 Walter Berns, "The Morality of Anger," in Hugo Bedau, ed., *For Capital Punishment* (New York: Basic Books, 1979).

Berns also defends legal moralism as a theory of what actions should be illegal. In one of his early works he supports bans on pornography, public profanity, and indecency on the ground that the law should lend support to the moral dispositions of the people, promote virtue, and habituate good citizens to right action.[13] In principle one could adopt a 'legal moralist' conception of retribution – holding that punishment involves morally blaming the wrongdoer – without being a legal moralist in identifying what actions should be illegal. One could take the position that we punish to morally blame only those who harm others. In contrast, a Mabbott-type retributivist probably could not consistently deny that we punish to express moral indignation while also holding that the legislature should decide which actions to make illegal on the basis of whether society regards those actions to be immoral.

Kant and Hegel fall somewhere in between the poles of Mabbott and Berns. Mabbott explicitly distinguishes his theory of punishment from Hegel's precisely because Hegel sees an essential connection between punishment and moral or social wrongdoing, whereas for Mabbott the criminal is not a bad person, just someone who broke a rule (154). But neither Kant nor Hegel are necessarily legal moralists in the usual sense – neither necessarily thinks that we should legally punish individuals who caused no harm or violated no rights. Neither theorist explicitly addressed that issue, which does not seem to have drawn the focus of political theorists until later in the 19th century. Still, while Kant and Hegel do not defend the liberal position that philosophers such as John Stuart Mill and Joel Feinberg eventually come to take, and which I will discuss soon – that the state may use coercion only to prevent someone from causing harm (or for Feinberg, harm or offense) to others – they do adopt a political theory according to which the state enforces rights, and it is consistent with their position that the criminal law should target *only* those who violate rights. That position is distinct from the legal moralist position that the state may punish those who act immorally even if they did not violate a right. Kant believes that suicide is morally wrong and probably believed that encouraging someone to commit suicide is also morally wrong. In his 'Doctrine of Virtue', a part of the *Metaphysics of Morals* devoted to moral as opposed to legal principles, he even characterizes killing oneself as a crime (MM 422). But that need not mean he would condone the state's use of coercion to legally punish those who attempt or encourage suicide. I am not certain there is sufficient evidence from their writings to hazard a guess as to precisely where Hegel

13 Walter Berns, *Freedom, Virtue, and the First Amendment* (Baton Rouge: LSU Press, 1957), esp. pp. 93, 164, 226–7, 238–9, 241.

or Kant stand in the continuum between Mabbott and Berns, or to determine what their position would be regarding legal moralism as a theory that criminal laws should target immoral conduct that does not violate rights. But what is clear is that those retributivists who would most insist on punishing Ms. Carter – assuming she acted badly – are the legal moralists.

At this point it would be helpful to review where we are in the overall argument. I have argued that the retributivist would have reason to punish Ms. Carter if she culpably violated a law. For Mabbott-type retributivists, merely the fact that she broke a law provides all the reason we need to punish her. We punish her not to express blame, but because punishment is a corollary of having criminal laws. For retributivists like Hegel, the interest in punishing Ms. Carter would be to provide justice and vindicate the law. But if they agreed that Ms. Carter did not violate the law against involuntary manslaughter, Mabbott, and arguably Kant and Hegel, would have no reason to think she should be punished.

Still, some retributivists who fall on the 'Berns' side of the retributivist continuum might argue that we ought to legally punish Ms. Carter on the assumptions that in encouraging Conrad to kill himself she acted immorally, and that we ought to have laws that prohibit immoral conduct. In chapter 5 I will consider the former assumption. In the rest of this chapter I focus on the latter assumption. Should we have criminal laws targeting those who act immorally even if they do not cause harm or violate a legally enforceable right? This is a purely speculative question since no such law existed in Massachusetts, and it would be unfair and violate accepted legal principles to punish someone for doing something that we think ought to be against the law but at the time was not, as they would have had no notice that what they did would subject them to legal punishment. Legal moralists such as Berns could want such a law and could support punishment of Ms. Carter for violating it if it had been in place. But I now will argue that there are powerful reasons to reject legal moralism as a theory of what conduct should be illegal.

The case against legal moralism

In his dissent in *Bowers v. Hardwick*, Justice Blackmun argues against laws that make conduct illegal merely because by custom it has been regarded as immoral – in this instance private, consensual sodomy between men.[14] Justice Blackmun cites Justice Holmes: "[i]t is revolting to have no better

14 *Bowers v. Hardwick*, 478 U.S. 186 (1986); later overturned in *Lawrence v. Texas*, 539 U.S. 558 (2003).

reason for a rule of law than that it was laid down in the time of Henry IV" (478 U.S. at 199). Of course not all laws that express the people's moral dispositions are out of date or based merely on custom. There are reasons other than blind adherence to custom for thinking it wrong to encourage others to end their lives. However, as Justice Blackmun notes, "reasonable people may differ" about whether conduct is immoral (478 U.S. at 212).

Justice Blackmun concedes that if the Georgia statute at issue in *Bowers* banned public sex acts instead of private sexual conduct, the law would be permitted. He doesn't explain the distinction in detail, but it is not a difficult one to see: public sex acts are likely to offend others, and the state may have an interest in prohibiting conduct that deeply offends, even if it does not harm. Such public behavior might inhibit others from pursuing their aims. But two men having sex in private does not. Justice Blackmun draws on an idea that is central to classical liberalism: I should have the liberty to pursue my own aims as I think best so long as I leave others with a similar liberty to pursue their own aims.[15] If my conduct harms or offends others, the state has an interest in regulating it in order to protect the interests of others; but if my conduct is 'self-regarding' – if it does not keep others from pursuing their aims – then the state should not interfere with my liberty on the assumption that it knows better than I do how I should live my life. As John Stuart Mill writes in defending a principle of this sort, "if a person possesses any tolerable amount of common sense and experience, his own mode of laying out his existence is the best, not because it is the best in itself, but because it is his own mode."[16]

Mill and later generations of political theorists attempted to clarify this idea by developing various 'liberty-limiting principles' to determine when my pursuit of my aims improperly inhibits others from pursuing theirs. This project has resulted in a sizable literature that I cannot do justice to here, and so I will provide just brief summaries of a few of the leading principles, all of which are opposed to legal moralism.

There are obvious cases in which we should limit an individual's liberty. Serial murderers shouldn't have the liberty to pursue their passion of killing as this would prevent their victims from pursuing any of their aims. But two men having sex in private victimizes no one; it might upset others who found out about it; and if one of the men was cheating on his jilted lover

15 See Jeremy Waldron, "Toleration and Reasonableness," in Catriona McKinnon and Dario Castiglione, eds., *Culture of Toleration in Diverse Societies* (Manchester: Manchester University Press, 2003).

16 John Stuart Mill, "On Liberty," *Collected Works of J.S. Mill* (Toronto: University of Toronto Press, 1977), 3:7 [Hereafter OL; references are to chapter: paragraph].

it might hurt that person. But the liberty we must leave to others does not include a liberty not to be upset or have one's feelings hurt.

In *On Liberty*, Mill made the case that given the importance of liberty to individuals and to society collectively, the state should be permitted to limit liberty only for a compelling purpose, and he defined this purpose as preventing harm to others, where harming others involves more than merely upsetting their feelings. Mill's 'harm principle' holds that

> the only purpose for which power can be rightfully exercised over any member of a civilised community, against his will, is to prevent harm to others. His own good, either physical or moral, is not a sufficient warrant . . . Over himself, over his own body and mind, the individual is sovereign.
>
> (OL 1:9)

Leaving aside some controversial passages in *On Liberty* in which his position may be ambiguous, such as OL 5:7 on 'offences against decency', on Mill's view we should be free to harm ourselves or offend others without fear of legal punishment. We can use forms of non-legal punishment such as exhortation to discourage people from acting badly, without having to resort to legal punishment – though Mill also cautions against the conforming force of such social coercion (OL 4:6, 11). The harm principle is opposed to legal moralism because the legal moralist seeks to punish conduct that does not cause harm.

One might think that we needn't resort to legal moralism to punish Ms. Carter, because her conduct would be prohibited by the harm principle. By encouraging Conrad to kill himself she at least contributed to if not caused his death, death being the ultimate harm one can suffer. I rejected that argument in chapter 3 and return to it now. As Mill himself suggests, to harm someone is to injure "the interests" of another which "ought to be considered as rights" (OL 4:3). If I merely disappoint you or even hurt you, I have not harmed you insofar as you have no right not to be disappointed or hurt. Someone I love, for example, does not harm me in not returning my love, as I have no right to their love.[17] Nor can I be said to harm someone who asks me to assault them, as they have waived their right not to be assaulted. Michelle did nothing to violate any right of Conrad. Conrad had no right not to be advised, encouraged, or even spoken to forcefully. He had a right not to be coerced – a right that the law against involuntary manslaughter in effect enforces – but I have argued that he was not coerced. Michelle might

17 Cf. Joel Feinberg, *Harm to Others* (Oxford: Oxford University Press, 1984), ch. 1.

be said to have harmed Conrad if she caused him to die and he did not consent to his dying; if Michelle had pushed Conrad into a poison-filled truck against his will she would have violated his right to his life and harmed him. But that is not what happened.

Joel Feinberg has suggested that we widen the range of conduct that the state may prohibit. He argues that a liberal political theory is consistent with allowing state coercion of those whose conduct not merely harms but offends others. The offenses that Feinberg would be willing to have the state restrict must be serious and not a mere inconvenience; they must have intensity, durability, not be easily avoided, and witnesses must not have consented to view them. According to the offense principle that Feinberg defends, the state would not punish me even if I do something that is profoundly offensive such as defacing a flag or mutilating a corpse merely if others have the 'bare knowledge' of what I did. To offend you, my conduct must violate a right you have.[18] Feinberg's offense-to-others principle, then, like Mill's harm principle, would not support punishment of Ms. Carter, as Ms. Carter violated no right. Like the harm principle, the offense principle is opposed to the principle of legal moralism, according to which we may punish conduct that goes against the moral dispositions of society even if it violates no right.

Sarah Conly has provided some persuasive arguments in favor of another liberty-limiting principle, which she calls coercive paternalism, according to which the state may use coercion to prevent us from harming ourselves.[19] Her position, too, is very different than the position staked out by legal moralists. Legal moralism holds that if an individual's aims are not what society regards as appropriate, the individual's liberty may be restricted. It assumes there are some aims that are virtuous and objectively good that the state may force us to pursue. But coercive paternalism does not presume that. Conly argues that given our susceptibility to making cognitive errors, state intervention is justified to prevent us from mistakenly choosing the wrong means for achieving our ends (43). By increasing the likelihood that we will make instrumentally rational decisions, coercive paternalism lets us get better results and better meet our objectives (36, 178–80). Coercive paternalism wouldn't support laws preventing someone from ending their life knowingly and with due deliberation if that is their aim. But it might support the use of state coercion to prevent someone from impulsively taking their own life; and it could support laws preventing someone from coercively inciting

18 Joel Feinberg, *Offense to Others* (Oxford: Oxford University Press, 1985), pp. 49, 68.

19 Sarah Conly, *Against Autonomy: Justifying Coercive Paternalism* (New York: Cambridge University Press, 2013).

another to commit suicide, as coercion could prevent us from achieving our objectives.

In contrast to each of these liberty-limiting principles, legal moralism holds that our liberty may be restricted not merely to prevent us from harming or offending others, or even harming ourselves, but to keep us from acting in ways that society regards as immoral.[20] What I take to be a fatal objection to legal moralism is that it allows a majority to impose its moral convictions on everyone in society even though people may legitimately hold conflicting convictions. Such impositions fail to take into account a central feature of a modern liberal society: the fact of pluralism.

Take the case where the majority enacts a law prohibiting assisted suicide. As I will discuss in chapter 5, our attitudes toward suicide may be shaped by our views about whether our life is ours to control or whether there is a higher power to which we are accountable; they may depend on our religious and philosophical commitments, including our conception of what happens when we die. Such underlying beliefs may be part of what John Rawls calls a 'comprehensive doctrine'.[21] A religious person who believes all life is sacred and given to us by God so that it is not ours to take away may regard suicide, and any actions that assist in suicide, to be wrongs of the highest magnitude. But someone who denies that humans owe anything to a higher power, and who believes that some lives are not worth living, may view those who assist in a suicide in a more positive light. Laws prohibiting assisted suicide impose one comprehensive doctrine – perhaps one rooted in a particular religious tradition – on everyone in that society, even those who adhere to a different religion or to none at all. This violates the requirement that the state remain neutral between different comprehensive doctrines, in recognition of the fact of pluralism – the fact that liberal democratic societies include people with different conceptions of the life worth pursuing.

Rawls notes that after the 'Wars of Religion' that arose following the Reformation, modern democratic regimes developed a principle of toleration to avoid regressing to a society torn by religious and other ideological conflicts. This principle of toleration requires that our conception of justice and our laws "must allow for a diversity of general and comprehensive doctrines, and for the plurality of conflicting, and indeed incommensurable, conceptions of the meaning, value and purpose of human life."[22] A liberty-limiting principle such as the harm principle seeks to ensure the conditions of a free society in

20 Patrick Devlin, *The Enforcement of Morals* (New York: Oxford University Press, 1965).

21 John Rawls, *Political Liberalism* (New York: Columbia University Press, 1996).

22 John Rawls, "The Idea of an Overlapping Consensus," *Oxford Journal of Legal Studies* 7(1):1–25 (1987); at p. 4.

which all its citizens can pursue their aims to a reasonable degree. But legal moralism permits the coercion of those who do not share the comprehensive doctrine of the majority. Even coercive paternalism, as defended by Conly, respects individual liberty in a way that legal moralism does not. To punish someone for assisting another in voluntarily ending their life because we believe suicide is wrong and that it is immoral to contribute to this wrong would be to impose our own comprehensive doctrine on everyone, and this a liberal democratic society recognizing the fact of pluralism must not do.[23]

If we reject legal moralism, as I think we should, there may be little reason left for a retributivist to legally punish Ms. Carter.

Utilitarian purposes of punishment

Utilitarians see the primary purpose of punishment not as expressing blame or meting out justice, but as making society better off by reducing future crime. For the utilitarian, we ask not whether Ms. Carter deserves to be blamed, but whether she needs to be incapacitated, or deterred, or whether she should be punished to set an example for others so that they do not encourage people to commit suicide.

Utilitarianism is a philosophy guided by the principle of utility, which, as articulated by one of its early and leading proponents, Jeremy Bentham, "approves or disapproves of every action whatsoever, according to the tendency which it appears to have to augment or diminish the happiness of the party whose interest is in question."[24] Should I keep my promise? The utilitarian would decide by calculating the pleasures and pains that would result if I did, and if the pleasure outweighs the pain, I should; otherwise I should not. Bentham claims that the utilitarian calculation guides all our decisions, including our decision whether to punish (PML 7:1).

For Bentham, the purpose of punishment is to discourage crimes, or 'mischiefs'. A crime produces a 'primary mischief' and a 'secondary mischief' (PML 12:3). If I am robbed I suffer a primary mischief, and so do people who rely on me for support. Society sustains secondary mischief because the level of 'danger' and 'alarm' has been increased (PML 12:5). The 'danger' is that by committing the crime, the criminal suggests to others that it is feasible to do so, increasing the risk of imitation. 'Alarm' refers

23 In chapter 5 I return to this theory of 'liberal pluralism' and explain why it is not self-contradictory to defend it while insisting that everyone accept its assumptions.

24 Jeremy Bentham, *An Introduction to the Principles of Morals and Legislation* (New York: Hafner Press, 1948) (1789), 1:2 [Hereafter PML; references are to chapter: section]. Parts of this section draw on Tunick, *Punishment*, ch. 3.

to the increased fear we experience from this prospect (PML 12:8). Punishment increases social utility by decreasing both sorts of mischief (PML 13:1). Punishment is itself a mischief, since it inflicts pain, and so we should avoid using it except when needed to prevent some greater evil (PML 13:2).

Punishment increases social utility mainly by deterring. By punishing Ms. Carter we would deter her from repeating what she did in the future – this is individual deterrence; and more significantly, by punishing her others will see that they will face punishment if they imitate what she did and will be deterred from doing so – this is general deterrence. Punishment can decrease future crime also by incapacitating criminals. If we imprisoned Ms. Carter for 20 years and denied her the ability to communicate with others, that is 20 years she presumably would not pose a danger.

If punishing someone would have no deterrent or incapacitation benefit, then on Bentham's view we should not punish them. Bentham says, for example, that punishing infants or the insane may not be warranted, not because they are not culpable, but because they could not be deterred (PML 13:9). Bentham gives numerous other cases 'unmeet for punishment'. We should not punish when doing so would be groundless, inefficacious, unprofitable, too expensive, or needless, as when we could prevent mischiefs in some cheaper way (PML 13:3).

The utilitarian would ask whether punishing Ms. Carter would efficiently prevent mischiefs. It seems unlikely that Ms. Carter needs to be incapacitated. She could contribute to Conrad's death only because of their unique relationship and his predispositions, and the probability of her ever being in a similar situation may be quite low. The same reasoning suggests that it is unlikely Ms. Carter needs to be deterred. But even if I am wrong about that, it is not clear to what extent someone in Ms. Carter's position would be deterrable. Ms. Carter may have had sensible utilitarian reasons for encouraging Conrad to kill himself. She had repeatedly tried to get him help, to no avail, and he seemed to be truly miserable, so suicide may have been the only option she saw to end his pain. A utilitarian should take into account the disutility of Conrad's death not just to Conrad but to his family and loved ones – though it may be unlikely their disutility could outweigh that of a person who would live out their life in pain and misery, a point I return to in chapter 5. But in any case, Michelle did, by rationalizing that Conrad's mother was aware of his pain and eventually the family would understand that he was better off. She may have had a questionable utilitarian reason as well: that Conrad would be happier in heaven. Of course if she were faced with a threat of severe punishment, then she might have recalculated the net utility of encouraging Conrad to kill himself, which is precisely what the utilitarian legislator has in mind in using criminal laws and punishment as a tool to increase overall social utility. However, she might have genuinely believed Conrad would be happy in heaven, and that she would someday join him there, in which case the threat of legal punishment might not be efficacious. Others who encourage friends to commit suicide may be similarly resistant to the threat of punishment if they are driven by their own sense of what is right.

We may doubt that Ms. Carter correctly calculated the net utility of Conrad's suicide. We may wonder, for example, how one can be sure Conrad would not have eventually received successful therapy. Moreover, even if Michelle made an accurate assessment, there is a version of utilitarianism according to which we still might be justified in punishing her.

Rule utilitarianism holds that in deciding what to do we should not simply consider the costs and benefits of the act we contemplate. In contrast to the act utilitarian, who holds that the rightness or wrongness of an action is to be judged by the goodness or badness of its results, the rule utilitarian holds that the rightness or wrongness of an action is to be judged by the goodness or badness of the consequences not of the action, but of a rule that everyone should perform the action in like circumstances. For example, suppose you want to get into law school, and you offer me, your undergraduate professor, $2500 if I give you an A for your paper rather than the D it deserves.[25] The act utilitarian might tell me to take the money if it's clear nobody will find out about it and I won't live the rest of my life in fear of getting caught. (There might be other ways an act utilitarian works out the calculation that lead to the opposite outcome.) But rule utilitarians would approach the question differently. They would ask whether there is more social utility in a rule that people should be graded based on merit or in a rule that they should be graded based on their willingness to pay. They are likely to prefer the former rule, in part because it would make it more likely that future professionals had the skills to be effective at their jobs; and once we agree on that rule for utilitarian reasons, instructors would not be free to depart from it on particular occasions.[26] Returning to the Carter case, one might think there is greater overall utility in adhering to a rule that prohibits individuals from encouraging others to commit suicide, even if on some occasions encouraging someone to kill themselves would increase utility. Such a rule might promote respect for human life and have other residual benefits. In chapter 5 I will challenge the rule-utilitarian argument.

25 I borrow the example of grade bargaining from Kenneth Kipnis, "Criminal Justice and the Negotiated Plea," *Ethics* 86(2):93–106 (1976); at pp. 104–5.

26 Cf. John Rawls, "Two Concepts of Rules," *Philosophical Review* 64(1):3–32 (1955), discussed in chapter 5.

Leaving aside rule utilitarianism until then, and even if Ms. Carter had good utilitarian intentions, if she miscalculated the net utility of Conrad's suicide, and if we agree that her encouragement contributed to Conrad's death, regardless of whether it was the morally or legally relevant cause, then the utilitarian has a reason for punishing Ms. Carter: to deter others from taking actions that could similarly contribute to bad consequences.

But there are several objections to that position, some of which may lead us to doubt that the utilitarian argument for punishing Ms. Carter to deter others is weighty enough to override competing interests in free speech and privacy. One objection has to do with the assumption that Conrad's suicide resulted in net disutility, and so I will defer to my discussion of that assumption in chapter 5.

A second objection is that even if punishing Ms. Carter would deter others from encouraging suicide – perhaps others who, unlike Michelle, coerce vulnerable victims – we still need to consider the consequences to free speech and privacy if we make it a crime to contribute to another's suicide through one's words. This weighing is required by the principle of utility itself. The utilitarian decides what actions to take based on a calculation of the action's benefits and costs. Bentham recognizes the benefit punishment can have in deterring mischief, but he also recognizes the pain punishment causes and the expense it incurs, and his position is that we should punish only if the benefit exceeds the pain and expense. It seems unlikely that the benefit in punishing Ms. Carter would exceed the substantial, even staggering costs to free speech and privacy if we were to hold people accountable for the words they share in private with those to whom they are in trusting relationships, or if we hold authors or search engine providers accountable for actions people take based on the information they provide. Ms. Carter is probably not in need of deterrence or incapacitation – or if she is, those benefits could be achieved in a cheaper way by monitoring or counseling her rather than putting her in prison. The benefit of deterring others from manipulating the vulnerable into taking their own lives might be met by punishing only those who truly coerce and not those who merely encourage or assist someone to carry out their free and informed decision to die.

But the more that suicide laws are conditional on judgments about causation and coercion, the more uncertain it is whether one's conduct will be deemed illegal, and this leads to a third objection, which involves a dilemma. If deterrence is to work, people must know whether their actions are illegal. A bright-line rule such as 'never encourage suicide' would put those who encourage suicide on notice that their activity is illegal, whereas a rule more tailored to prohibiting only behavior that has disutility – such as 'do not recklessly cause harm' – will create uncertainty. One reason punishing Ms. Carter for committing involuntary manslaughter is unlikely to effectively deter others is, as I noted in chapter 3, that the law doesn't provide clear guidance as to what constitutes recklessly causing harm; deciding which of many causes of a suicide to single out as legally relevant involves a moral judgment that requires us to weigh many factors. When the law fails to provide clear guidance, people are not on notice that their behavior is illegal.[27] If I am uncertain that my behavior will be construed as causing harm and therefore as violating the law, I am less likely to be deterred by that law.[28] But if we adopt the bright-line rule we will deter too much.

There is a final objection to punishing Ms. Carter to deter others. Kant argues that man, and in general every rational being, exists as an end in themselves, not merely as an object to be used for the good of others.[29] To punish Ms. Carter not because we think she caused Conrad's death and deserves punishment but because she contributed to a bad consequence that we want to discourage in the future would be to use her as a tool for our social objectives, not unlike if the state were to conduct dangerous medical experiments on a prisoner. This fails to respect her dignity as a human being. Hegel also objects to using punishment as a deterrent, though he focuses on how it treats not the recipient, but those who the state hopes to deter. To justify punishment by using it as a threat, he says, "is like raising one's stick at a dog; it means treating a human being like a dog instead of respecting his honor and freedom" (PR 99 Addition).

This objection would fall flat if Ms. Carter deserved punishment, for then we would not be treating her merely as a means or punishing her merely to deter others – but I have presented a case that she does not.

Conclusion

The retributivist has little reason to punish Ms. Carter: she did not clearly violate a law, or violate rights, or cause harm. A legal moralist may want her to be punished to express anger at her apparent callousness, but there are powerful objections to using legal punishment to impose the moral sensibilities of one subset of society on everyone else. On a utilitarian theory, it might be beneficial to punish someone for contributing to bad consequences even if they aren't the morally relevant cause of those consequences and aren't morally blameworthy. But punishing Ms. Carter for her words would

27 It appears Ms. Carter became aware that she could go to jail only after Conrad died and she learned that police were interested in her text messages, suggesting she was not previously on notice that what she did may have been illegal. See her text to Samantha Boardman of July 21, 10:29pm, cited in chapter 1.

28 See, e.g., Kaplow and Shavell, *Fairness v. Welfare*, ch. 6.

29 Immanuel Kant, *Groundwork of the Metaphysic of Morals*, tr. H.J. Paton (New York: Harper and Row, 1964), p. 95.

chill free speech and private interactions, and the principle of utility requires that those consequences be weighed against the interest in public safety; in addition, there are moral objections, raised by Kant and Hegel, to punishing someone merely so that others will be deterred; and finally, and most controversially, we need to ask if the conduct being deterred – encouraging others to commit suicide – necessarily decreases social utility – which I address in the next chapter.

5 Suicide laws

Overview

The texts between Michelle Carter and Conrad Roy revealed that Conrad was depressed and had attempted suicide before. Michelle expressed concern and tried to make him feel better about his life, but with no success. A psychiatrist who testified on Michelle's behalf suggested that over the years she knew him she was weighed down by his depression.[1] After encouraging him to seek help, she appears to have become frustrated, and may have sincerely reached the point of believing Conrad would be happier dead or, in her words, better off in heaven. For example, Michelle texts Conrad on July 1, 2014: "Jesus will take care of you babe, you'll be happy and protected in heaven. I just want you to finally be happy, so so happy. And if this is the only way you think you're gonna be happy, heaven will welcome you with open arms." Less than two weeks later, after Conrad used a water pump to release carbon monoxide gas into his truck while he sat inside, got scared, stepped out, and spoke with Michelle on the phone, she told him to get back in the toxic truck.

Justice Cordy of the Massachusetts Supreme Judicial Court insisted that the Carter case was not a case of euthanasia, or mercy killing, but was instead a "systematic campaign of coercion" to end Conrad's life.[2] He is of course right that Ms. Carter did not assist in euthanasia – Conrad was not terminally ill, about to die of natural causes, and Michelle did not simply hasten his death with good intentions in the same way that a loved one might pull the plug of a life-support device that is keeping a family member alive.[3] Yet Justice Cordy seems wrong to imply that Michelle acted with malice.

1 "Can Words Kill?", ABC's *20/20*, broadcast August 4, 2017.

2 *Commonwealth v. Carter*, 474 Mass. 624, 636 (2016).

3 Terminating one's life-sustaining treatment is 'passive euthanasia', which differs from voluntary active euthanasia, where an individual, usually a physician, ends a patient's life by some medical means such as injection: see Ezekiel Emanuel et.al., "Attitudes and Practices

If Ms. Carter sincerely believed Conrad would be better off ending his life, then in encouraging Conrad to kill himself, and saying 'get back in' the truck, did she act badly? Is encouraging or assisting suicide always wrong, and should doing so be illegal?

I argued in chapter 3 that Ms. Carter violated no laws. Massachusetts has no law against assisting in or encouraging suicide; and to be guilty of involuntary manslaughter she would have had to have a legal duty to intervene, or her words would have had to cause Conrad's death – but she had no legal duty, and she did not cause his death. But ought there to be a law against what she did? I will look critically at two lines of argument one might put forth in defense of such a law. The first is a utilitarian argument, introduced in chapter 4: that suicide is a bad consequence – it has disutility – and a law that punished those who encourage suicide could have a positive effect on society's overall utility even taking into account the disutility of punishing. I will cast doubt on this line of argument by questioning whether suicide is necessarily a bad consequence.

A second line of argument goes like this: in encouraging Conrad to kill himself and offering advice about how he could do so, Ms. Carter acted badly, and it is appropriate for the state to legally punish those who act badly. In chapter 4 I argued against the principle of legal moralism upon which this argument relies – that the state should use its coercive power to ensure that people conform to the moral sensibilities of the majority even when their conduct causes no harm or violates no legally enforceable right. In this chapter I challenge this line of argument in another way, by questioning whether Ms. Carter really did act badly.

I will focus on two distinct ways in which one might think Ms. Carter acted badly. First is the argument that may resonate with those who are most outraged by Ms. Carter's actions: that suicide is wrong, being a transgression against a higher law, and that anyone who assists in or encourages the commission of this wrong acts badly and deserves punishment. But suppose we reject that argument, and we allow that in particular cases suicide may not be wrong, as in cases where it results from a voluntary, deliberate choice of an individual living with incurable pain or inconsolable misery. Even in cases where suicide itself is not wrong, *encouraging* someone to commit suicide still might be wrong. According to the liberal principle of individual autonomy, individuals should have the liberty to make their own choices regarding important life decisions so long as their choices don't prevent others from exercising the same liberty. According to this principle, my assisting someone who freely makes an informed decision to kill themselves is

of Euthanasia and Physician-Assisted Suicide in the United States, Canada, and Europe," *JAMA* 316(1):79–90 (2016); at p. 80.

permissible because I do not limit but rather facilitate the individual's free choice; but my encouraging them to kill themselves may be wrong if I exert undue influence that makes the individual's choice no longer their own; or it may be wrong on other grounds if I had malevolent motives. After assessing the utilitarian argument, I turn to each of these other arguments. In my discussion I shall use the term 'suicide laws' to refer to laws that prohibit suicide or its assistance, advisement, or encouragement, though in the final section I shall emphasize the distinctions between these sorts of laws.

The utilitarian argument: is suicide always a bad consequence?

On the utilitarian approach, if Ms. Carter contributed to Conrad's death, then punishing her might be justified to deter others from also contributing to future suicides. By avoiding those bad consequences, society might be better off. In the next section I will discuss a theistic argument against suicide: that suicide is wrong because it transgresses a higher law that declares human life to be sacrosanct. But the utilitarian rejects the notion that there is a higher law, be it divine or natural, that dictates what is right and wrong. For the utilitarian, the only basis for saying that something is right or wrong is that it does or does not accord with the principle of utility. An action whose effect is to increase overall social utility is right; one that decreases overall utility is wrong. Jeremy Bentham writes that when so interpreted, the words "[r]ight and wrong . . . have a meaning: when otherwise, they have none."[4]

Leaving aside rule utilitarians, whose position I introduced in chapter 4 and will return to shortly, utilitarians are unlikely to regard every suicide as a bad consequence. A life of lingering pain would be worse than nonexistence, even taking into account indirect effects on family members or other loved ones the suicide leaves behind. Bentham is critical of laws against suicide, as well as the forfeiture laws existing in his day that deprived the remaining family members of their inheritance, because some individuals could rationally want to end their lives to cease their pain. Doing so, Bentham argues, would promote utility even when factoring in the disutility of those they leave behind. For the person contemplating suicide, "the prospect of the pain he shall suffer by continuing to live" affects him more than the pain it seems that those who depend on or care for him will endure by his death.[5]

4 Jeremy Bentham, *An Introduction to the Principles of Morals and Legislation* (New York: Hafner, 1948), 1:10.

5 Jeremy Bentham, "Principles of Penal Law," in Bowring, ed., *The Works of Jeremy Bentham* (New York: Russell and Russell, 1962), vol. 1, 2:4.

John Stuart Mill, another utilitarian, agrees with Bentham that death is not always a bad consequence. In his speech in defense of capital punishment Mill argues that "depriving [a man] of all that makes life desirable or valuable" can be worse than taking his life. Mill asks, "Is it, indeed, so dreadful a thing to die?" For Mill, "[i]t is not human life only [t]hat ought to be sacred to us, but human feelings. The human capacity of suffering is what we should cause to be respected, not the mere capacity of existing."[6] As did Bentham, Mill recognizes that some lives may be so filled with suffering that ending them would not be a bad consequence.

Bentham assumes that each of us knows better than anyone else whether our life is worth living; no one but me can better calculate my net pleasure or pain.[7] That assumption might seem questionable especially when applied to teenagers or young adults of Conrad's age. Shakespeare's *Romeo and Juliet* is so tragic because young Romeo's impulsive decision to poison himself was clearly the wrong decision. In hindsight he would agree it was the wrong decision were he still alive. We saw in chapter 4 that Sara Conly bases her defense of coercive paternalism on the fact that many of us make cognitive errors in judging which means are best suited to achieve our desired ends. Teenagers who are Conrad's age are particularly likely to make rash decisions that don't properly take into account consequences in the more distant future. For example, studies of cigarette smoking suggest that teenagers and young adults are especially prone to engage in harmful behavior because they incorrectly discount the future effects of smoking.[8] If Bentham is mistaken, and some individuals gravely err in assessing whether their life will be one of well-being or ill-being – terms Bentham uses in discussing suicide (Deontology, 130) – and if Conrad eventually received effective treatment for his depression, he might have lived another 70 or 80 years, raised a family, and lived a happy, worthwhile life.

But Conrad did not act impulsively over what he thought was the loss of a loved one, as did Romeo. He was not deciding between a momentary pleasure from nicotine intake and distant ill effects on his health that he was likely to discount too much. He was suffering and profoundly unhappy and had already been hospitalized and received treatment. The error one asserts that Conrad made is that he failed to see that his misery, suffering, and

6 J.S. Mill, "Speech in Favor of Capital Punishment," April 21, 1868, in Robson, ed., *Collected Works of J.S. Mill* (Toronto: University of Toronto Press, 1988), vol. 28, pp 269–70.

7 Jeremy Bentham, *Deontology: Together with a Table of the Springs of Action*, ed. Amnon Goldworth (Oxford: Oxford University Press, 1983), pp. 130–1. Bentham restricts this claim to calculations of my own well-being rather than of the net utility for society that might result from my actions; but in decisions about suicide he suggests this generally suffices.

8 See Pepita Barlow, et.al., "Time-Discounting and Tobacco Smoking: A Systematic Review and Network Analysis," *International Journal of Epidemiology* 46(3):860–9 (2017).

unhappiness during his last few years may one day have ended, and that he might still have had a future he would have wanted to live. But that does not seem to be the sort of cognitive error Conly wants the state paternalistically to protect us from, nor is it the same sort of cognitive error made by Romeo, or by teens who smoke cigarettes.

Let's compare Conrad's suicide to one of the most famous suicides recorded in history – though perhaps it is apocryphal. According to the Roman historian Livy, Sextus Tarquinius wanted to have Lucretia, the beautiful but chaste and devoutly religious wife of Collatinus, but could not get her to yield with his charm, or even after threatening to kill her. Lucretia valued her chastity more than her life. So Sextus then threatened not only to kill her but to slit the throat of a slave and put the dead slave's naked body by her side so that people would think Lucretia committed adultery with him. Concerned for her honor, only then did Lucretia yield. She then decided to take her own life, and did, but only after discussing her situation with others and duly deliberating. Even though she declares her heart was innocent, she explains that she does not want to be an "example for unchaste women to escape what they deserved." Lucretia's decision to take her own life has been sternly criticized by the likes of St. Augustine, who wonders why she killed herself if she really was innocent.[9] Her choice may look to some of us today as driven by a misguided sense of honor and a miscalculation both of what her reputation is likely to be and of the importance of reputation. Yet – and this is what I take Bentham's point to be – so long as she acted with deliberation and not, like Romeo, impulsively, who is anyone but Lucretia to say whether she can live with herself? Or whether Conrad can live with his pain or misery?[10]

Rule utilitarians might recognize Bentham's and Mill's point that for some people death is preferable to an existence filled with suffering or despair, yet still argue that suicide and its assistance or encouragement should be prohibited. As discussed in chapter 4, a rule utilitarian holds that the rightness or wrongness of an action is to be judged by the goodness or badness of the consequences of a rule that everyone should perform the action in like circumstances. Rule utilitarians might think there is greater overall utility enforcing a rule that requires respect for life than in leaving to each individual the choice of whether to take their own life. In making

9 Livy, *The Early History of Rome*, tr. Aubrey De Selincourt (New York: Penguin Books, 1960), pp. 98–100; and St. Augustine, *City of God* (New York: Penguin Books, 1972), Bk I, ch. 19.

10 This is not to deny that Sextus might still be a relevant cause of Lucretia's death, just as Stephenson was a relevant cause of Madge Oberholzer's suicide – see the discussion of *Stephenson v. State* in chapter 3.

this case they would not appeal to a higher law declaring all human life to be sacrosanct. Rather, they would argue that society is better off if people are habituated to respect human life. While on occasion this might mean that someone who is suffering must endure their pain, overall social utility is greater when the rule is enforced.

But the rule-utilitarian argument is problematic. Mill was not convinced by it in his speech in favor of capital punishment. He notes that "[m]uch has been said of the sanctity of human life, and the absurdity of supposing that we can teach respect for life by ourselves destroying it." Mill rejects that argument because it could be "brought against any punishment whatever."[11] If our goal is to encourage people to respect human life, Mill is suggesting, we shouldn't inflict pain on anyone, a prospect Mill apparently thinks is absurd.

But if we accept punishment as a tool to promote respect for human life, as do defenders of suicide laws, why not punish every action that is disrespectful, or that casts humans in an undignified light, or that condones violence? On the principle that we should disincentivize anything that might fuel an attitude of disrespect, we could punish insults, indignities, participants in boxing matches or any sport with violence, and possibly those participating in the system of wage labor, or who produce and distribute pornography, or even Three Stooges films. But many actions that appear to treat humans as objects to be used for the amusement or benefit of others have utility nevertheless. A rule that prohibited suicide to encourage respect for life would similarly be overbroad. Sometimes we respect human life by recognizing that some individuals are living a life so lacking in dignity and filled with pain that requiring them to linger on is inhumane.

The concern that a rule of 'no suicide' is overbroad points to a general objection to rule utilitarianism. Why worship rules that lead to bad outcomes on particular occasions?[12] Why not allow exceptions when warranted? John Rawls provides a reason in the case of rules that define or are constitutive of useful social practices, such as the rules of punishment or promising. According to his 'practice conception of rules', the rule 'punish only the guilty' defines punishment, distinguishing it from other practices we might adopt but do not as they would have less utility. Once we decide to adopt the practice of punishment, as opposed to alternatives that

11 Mill, "Speech in Favor of Capital Punishment," p. 270.

12 See J.J.C. Smart, "An Outline of a System of Utilitarian Ethics," in Smart and Williams, eds., *Utilitarianism: For and Against* (London: Cambridge University Press, 1973), p. 10; and C.L. Ten, *Crime, Guilt, and Punishment* (Oxford: Oxford University Press, 1987), ch. 4.

might allow for harsh treatment of the innocent, and we are inside the practice, we aren't free to make exceptions to that rule even if doing so would increase social utility. A judge can't say, "Although this defendant is innocent, I think it would be best on the whole if we punished him." The practice does not allow departures from the rules that constitute the practice. But the rule 'no suicide' is not constitutive of any social practice, and Rawls's 'practice conception of rules' would not apply to it.[13] Nor is it clear that a utilitarian would want to defend a rule 'no suicide'. That rule would be justified on the premise that all human life is sacrosanct, but that is not a principle that itself is clearly defensible on utilitarian grounds. Suicide laws would contribute to an overall increase in social utility if the 'no suicide' rule they enforce would deter suicide by people who would have lived a life of 'well-being' as opposed to 'ill-being'; but suicides often are committed by those who determine their life is not worth living. Using the formulation of rule utilitarianism I provided earlier, that we judge the rightness of an action based on the consequences of a rule that everyone should perform the action 'in like circumstances', we might say that people who are suffering or miserable are not in like circumstances and therefore are not bound by the rule. But then rule utilitarianism risks collapsing into act utilitarianism and might not support suicide laws as applied to many people who kill themselves.

Taking into account the other objections to the utilitarian account, discussed in chapter 4, the utilitarian line of argument in defense of suicide laws has little left to recommend it. Of course the utilitarian could want the state to devote substantial resources for suicide hotlines, counseling, education, and other measures, especially measures that preempt impulsive actions, and could support laws that deter bullying and other forms of coercion or manipulation.

Did Ms. Carter act badly in encouraging suicide?

The utilitarian defense of suicide laws – laws that prohibit suicide or its assistance, advisement, or encouragement – falters because suicide is not always a bad consequence. But a case for suicide laws may still be made on other grounds besides utilitarianism. One could argue that suicide is morally wrong, as is encouraging it, and according to the principle of legal moralism we should legally punish those who commit or contribute to a moral

13 John Rawls, "Two Concepts of Rules," *Philosophical Review* 64(1):3–32 (1955); for further explanation of this point see Mark Tunick, "Should We Aim for a Unified and Coherent Theory of Punishment?" *Criminal Law and Philosophy* 10(3):611–28 (2016).

wrong. I criticized the principle of legal moralism in chapter 4, and I will return to and expand upon that criticism after first turning my attention to the other assumption of this line of argument: is suicide morally wrong and in encouraging it did Michelle act badly?

The theistic and other arguments that suicide is wrong

Objections to suicide often rest on religious or philosophical convictions about the value or meaning of life. For some people, every human life is precious and sacrosanct. Kant, for example, regards suicide as abominable and inadmissible on moral grounds, because it "degrades human nature below the level of animal nature and so destroys it."[14] Kant argues that "suicide is in no circumstances permissible." The man who ends his life "treats his value as that of a beast . . . he is no longer a human being; he has made a thing of himself" (LE 151). After presenting these moral objections, Kant then examines suicide "from the standpoint of religion" in order to see it "in its true light" (LE 153), and argues that suicide opposes the purpose of man's Creator: "We have no right to offer violence to our nature's powers of self-preservation and to upset the wisdom of her arrangements." Human beings are "sentinels on earth," and "they may not leave their posts until relieved by another beneficent hand. God is our owner; we are His property" (LE 154). Kant thus gives a theistic objection to suicide, although on Kant's view suicide is not wrong because God forbids it arbitrarily; rather, "God has forbidden it because it is abominable in that it degrades man's inner worth below that of the animal creation" (LE 154). The theistic objection has been advanced by other important figures in the history of philosophy including John Locke, who declares that our lives belong to God and are not ours to take: "[man in a state of nature] has not liberty to destroy himself . . . for men being all the workmanship of one omnipotent [. . .] they are his property."[15]

The Scottish philosopher David Hume was not convinced by this argument. He asks, "why do you conclude that providence has placed me in this station? For my part I find that I owe my birth to a long chain of causes, of which many and even the principal depended upon voluntary actions of

14 Immanuel Kant, *Lectures on Ethics*, tr. Infield (London: Hackett, 1980), pp. 151–2 [Hereafter LE].

15 John Locke, *Second Treatise of Government* (Indianapolis: Hackett, 1980), Par. 6.

men."[16] Hume argues at this point from a deistic perspective: God put into operation general and immutable laws but is not interested in overseeing particular events, and instead entrusts men to their own judgment and discretion (Par. 7); but, Hume continues, even if providence guided all these causes, then it causes my suicide too and we can just as well conclude that "I am recalled from my station in the clearest and most express terms" (Par. 13).[17]

There are other reasons to object to suicide apart from the theistic argument that suicide is a transgression of our duty to God. One might argue that suicide violates our duty to our loved ones, who may rely upon us for support; or to our community, to whose cooperative schemes we have an obligation to contribute in return for the benefits we received from them. Hume is just as skeptical of these arguments. Most people who are tempted to suicide, Hume writes, are living a "miserable existence" the prolonging of which will provide no advantage; it may rather amount to a burden. Hume suggests that in these cases suicide may even be "laudable" (Par. 15). Hume agrees with Bentham and Mill that not all lives are worth living. Hume counted in this category lives "loaded with pain and sickness, with shame and poverty" (Par. 10) or in which "the horror of pain prevails over the love of life" (Par. 11).

Accepting suicide as a valid choice may seem to cheapen human life; it may make it seem as if the value of my life is determined by me alone, so that if I decide it is not worth anything anymore it really does not have any value; and that is a proposition that many people cannot accept. Yet the idea that some lives may be so painful or lacking in dignity that they are no longer worth living cannot be dismissed; nor can we dismiss the idea that the decision about whether I should continue my life must be left to me, and that I am not under the command of a higher power. People are bound to disagree about these questions. Rather than attempting to affirm or refute the theistic argument or Kant's supposed secular argument that suicide fails to respect the intrinsic value of human life, I will be content to assume that reasonable people can plausibly hold that suicide is not always wrong, and that there can be circumstances in which encouraging someone to commit suicide is not to act badly, such as when one has good motives and intentions and is not exerting undue or coercive pressure. The question we must then confront is what position the state should take on whether suicide or its encouragement or assistance is ever permissible: should the state use

16 David Hume, "On Suicide," in *Essays on Suicide and the Immortality of the Soul* (Basil: James Decker, 1799), Par. 13.

17 For criticism of Hume's arguments see G.R. McLean, "Hume and the Theistic Objection to Suicide," *American Philosophical Quarterly* 38(1):99–111 (2001).

the full panoply of its coercive powers – including laws, the police, courts, and prisons – to ensure that one side prevails on a controversial issue about which reasonable people disagree?

The liberal pluralist argument against suicide laws

As is apparent from debates concerning whether there is a right to end one's life with the assistance of a physician, reasonable people have argued forcefully that sometimes suicide, and assisting in suicide, may be justified. In the United States, suicide is no longer against the law, and with the Supreme Court decision of *Cruzan v. Director, Missouri Department of Health* there is a recognized right of an individual to refuse to continue the operation of life-support machines, although the state may demand clear and convincing evidence of the individual's wishes.[18] In light of *Cruzan*, one may assist someone who has decided to die by unplugging their life-support machine. But federal courts in the United States have as yet been unwilling to extend this 'right to die' to encompass a right to physician-assisted suicide (PAS), in which a doctor provides drugs for a terminally ill patient to self-administer with the patient's full consent.[19] This means that as of 2018, physician-assisted suicide is prohibited in the U.S. in all but six states that enacted legislation permitting it, though it is legal in Switzerland, the Netherlands, Belgium, Luxembourg, Colombia, and Canada, with the latter five countries also permitting active euthanasia, in which the physician administers the drug.[20]

When the U.S. Supreme Court was preparing to decide whether laws prohibiting physician-assisted suicide violate a fundamental constitutional right to make the decision about whether to end one's life for oneself, some leading American philosophers submitted a "Philosopher's Brief" in support of the individual's right to decide. They focused on the question of whether willing physicians should be permitted to assist a consenting, terminally ill patient – a very different set of circumstances than we are presented with in the Carter case – but their argument applies to a wider set of cases. They claimed that individuals can make a reasonable, considered judgment that even if they were not in pain, their life may be so filled with anguish that they would be better off ending it. They then argued that regardless of whether we agree with the individual's decision, it should be theirs to make: "The Constitution insists that people must be free to make these deeply personal decisions for themselves and must not be forced to end their lives in a

18 497 U.S. 261 (1990).
19 *Washington v. Glucksberg*, 521 U.S. 702 (1997), and *Vacco v. Quill*, 521 U.S. 793 (1997).
20 Emanuel et.al., "Attitudes and Practices," p. 80.

way that appalls them [referring to being intubated, helpless, and sedated], just because that is what some majority thinks proper."[21]

In a later section I will discuss a specific constitutional argument against suicide laws: that insofar as these laws are grounded in a religious view that suicide is wrong, in enacting them the state would violate the principle that state and church must be separate, a principle enforced by the First Amendment's Establishment Clause. But the idea that the state should not enact suicide laws because in doing so it would be favoring one set of controversial beliefs over others can be defended without relying on the First Amendment.

The theistic objection to suicide, that our lives are given to us by God and are not ours to abandon, relies on a religious conviction that is part of what John Rawls refers to as a comprehensive doctrine.[22] Someone who does not share that religious conviction and who denies there is a higher power may well believe that suicide can sometimes be justified and should not be prohibited by the state. Suicide laws impose one particular comprehensive doctrine on everyone in that society, but according to the principle of liberal pluralism the state must not favor one comprehensive doctrine over another.

Liberal pluralism assumes that all human beings are free and equal and should be afforded the liberty to pursue their aims; but because we are equal, the liberty we are given must be consistent with everyone else having a similar liberty. Kant expresses this idea in claiming that there is but one innate right all human beings have: "freedom (independence from being constrained by another's choice), insofar as it can coexist with the freedom of every other in accordance with a universal law" (MM 237). Theorists have developed different formulations to characterize the liberty we each should have that is compatible with everyone else having an equal liberty. For example, John Stuart Mill says we should be free to do as we please so long as we do not harm others. Jeremy Waldron says a liberal society should permit a range of actions that is adequate for each individual to pursue their ends as long as these actions are compatible with others in society adequately pursuing their ends.[23] Sara Conly's principle of coercive paternalism would qualify Mill's harm principle by allowing limitations of our liberty to ensure that we aren't inhibited from realizing our aims

21 Ronald Dworkin, Thomas Nagel, Robert Nozick, John Rawls, Judith Jarvis Thomson, et.al., "Assisted Suicide: The Philosophers' Brief," *New York Review of Books* (March 27, 1997).

22 John Rawls, *Political Liberalism* (New York: Columbia University Press, 1996).

23 Jeremy Waldron, "Toleration and Reasonableness," in Catriona McKinnon and Dario Castiglione, eds., *Culture of Toleration in Diverse Societies* (Manchester: Manchester University Press, 2003).

by cognitive errors about what means will let us best realize our aims.[24] While the specific formulations differ in important ways, there is a common underlying idea: we should be free to pursue our aims so long as others are given an equal liberty to pursue theirs. We should have the liberty to make choices consistent with our religious or philosophical convictions, so long as this does not prevent others from doing the same, and so long as we don't require others to adhere to our convictions. Christians, Muslims, or Jews must not force others to comply with the requirements of Christianity, Islam, or Judaism.

The principle of liberal pluralism itself is part of a comprehensive doctrine that values individual autonomy and equality. That doctrine is not shared by everyone: there are people who believe only some should be free, or that individuals with different genders or religions or ethnicities are not equal. Liberal pluralists hold that a comprehensive doctrine should not be imposed on others yet insist that everyone's liberty should be restricted to comply with the requirements of liberal pluralism. While that may seem to be self-contradictory, liberal pluralism is intended to apply only to societies that share the fundamental assumption that humans are free and equal. Liberal pluralism, in allowing state coercion to prevent harm to others, or some such principle, sets basic ground rules necessary for people with different comprehensive doctrines to live together; but they must accept the basic assumption that humans are free and equal.

An example: oyako shinju

According to liberal pluralism, the state should not interfere with Conrad's free and informed decision on whether to kill himself – that is his decision to make. But the state should not be neutral and may intervene with force to keep us from harming others or perhaps preventing them in other ways from pursuing their aims. The following example illustrates the liberty that liberal pluralism does and does not allow.

Fumiko Kimura was a mother living in California with her two young children. After she learned that her husband kept a mistress, she resolved to kill herself. According to her Japanese culture, leaving her children behind without a mother would subject them to ridicule and shame, and according to her set of beliefs they would be better off joining her in an afterlife. So she attempted *oyako shinju*, or mother-child suicide, leading her 6-month-old daughter and 4-year-old son into the Pacific Ocean. She was rescued by a

24 Sarah Conly, *Against Autonomy: Justifying Coercive Paternalism* (New York: Cambridge University Press, 2013).

bystander, but her children drowned. She was at first charged with two counts of murder. The Japanese community petitioned to reduce these charges, arguing that Ms. Kimura should be tried not by the standards and law of the United States, but by the standards she was raised to live by. In Japan *oyako shinju* is not uncommon and is not treated as a serious offense given its meaning within Japanese culture. Ms. Kimura was eventually convicted of voluntary manslaughter and sentenced to one year in jail, five years' probation, and ordered to undergo counseling.[25]

Ms. Kimura might claim that according to her set of beliefs she did not harm her children. But a liberal pluralist rejects that claim. Liberal pluralists need not declare Ms. Kimura's beliefs about an afterlife and the importance of avoiding shame to be false, and they may even take those beliefs into account in deciding her culpability and the amount of punishment she deserves.[26] But they insist that the state may prevent individuals from denying others the opportunity to exercise their liberty. Ms. Kimura should be free to take her own life; but she must not impose her views on her children by killing them. Prohibiting *oyako shinju* may keep Ms. Kimura from achieving an aim she believes is important, but according to liberal pluralism certain aims that constrain others are impermissible.

The First Amendment Establishment Clause objection to suicide laws

If the claim that suicide is wrong rests on religious doctrine, suicide laws would not only be suspect according to the political theory of liberal pluralism but they may violate the First Amendment Establishment Clause, which prohibits government from making any "law respecting an establishment of religion, or prohibiting the free exercise thereof." The 'no establishment of religion' provision has been interpreted to mean that the state must remain neutral when faced with religious controversies. According to the first two prongs of Chief Justice Burger's *Lemon* test, it requires that laws "have a secular legislative purpose," and their "principal or primary effect must be one that neither advances nor inhibits religion."[27] According to Justice O'Conner's 'endorsement test', it requires that a law must not have the purpose or effect of endorsing religion; if it did, this would send a message to non-adherents that they are outsiders.[28]

25 *People v. Kimura*, A-091133, Superior Court of Los Angeles; reported in *National Law Journal*, August 5, 1985, p. 1; November 4, 1985; and April 27, 1989.

26 As I argue in Tunick, "Can Culture Excuse Crime? Evaluating the Inability Thesis," *Punishment and Society* 6:395–409 (2004).

27 *Lemon v. Kurtzman*, 403 U.S. 602, 612 (1971).

28 *Lynch v. Donnelly*, 465 U.S. 668 (1984).

Edward Rubin has argued that laws making it a crime to assist in suicide are a coercive imposition of a Christian-based morality and therefore violate the Establishment Clause.[29] Rubin notes that among the ancient Greeks and Romans there was a classical morality that sometimes saw suicide as a virtuous action that preserved a person's honor. Then there was a shift with the rise of Christian morality. The early Christian Church didn't explicitly prohibit suicide, and sometimes glorified martyrdom. But later in its history a strict opposition to suicide arose – Rubin cites as an example the work of St. Thomas Aquinas, who argues that decisions about life or death belong to God alone (776). Rubin notes yet a later shift in the late 18th and early 19th centuries to a modern morality of self-fulfillment that emphasizes individualism: we should be able to lead a life that satisfies our aspirations and desires (778). This modern morality is "solicitous of life" and views its sacrifice for honor as "wasteful pride," but also acknowledges that suicide could be an appropriate though not obligatory response "when there is no further possibility of living a fulfilling life" (779–80). According to this modern morality, suicide need not be morally condemned, unless perhaps the suicides leave behind others who depended on them, which is a condemnation not of suicide per se (780) but of the suicides' failure to make plans to provide for their dependents. The Christian view that suicide is wrong can conflict with the modern morality, and, Rubin argues, when states enact suicide laws they take sides in this debate and therefore violate the Establishment Clause.

Some might wonder why, if the state permitted assisted suicide, would it not also be taking sides? It is not difficult to respond to this question. The Establishment Clause prevents the government from coercing people to comply with religious requirements. Without suicide laws, individuals facing the moral question of whether to assist in suicide would no longer have to factor in the threat of government coercion. It is only when the government enacts laws that threaten to punish certain decisions and therefore change the costs and benefits an individual must account for in their moral calculation that the state violates the principle of neutrality. Only without such laws are people free to make their own decisions, subject to the coercive effects of public opinion and social pressure to be sure, but without the state essentially taking the decision out of their hands. The state should leave us free to make decisions so long as our decisions don't violate the rights of others. Public accommodation laws force some business owners to violate their religious convictions by catering to same-sex couples seeking

29 Edward Rubin, "Assisted Suicide, Morality, and Law: Why Prohibiting Assisted Suicide Violates the Establishment Clause," *Vanderbilt Law Review* 63:763–811 (2010).

to exercise their right to marry.[30] Such laws may seem to violate the principle of neutrality just like suicide laws. But they can be distinguished. The public accommodation law prevents the business owner from violating a legally recognized right – a right not to be discriminated against; but a law prohibiting assisted suicide does not, as the person who assists in a suicide violates no right.

Rubin's claim that suicide laws violate the Establishment Clause is convincing only if these laws necessarily take sides in a religious debate. If suicide can be regarded as wrong on non-religious grounds, the First Amendment objection – though not the objection that appeals to the broader principle of liberal pluralism – falls away. Earlier we saw that there can be non-religious objections to suicide. The rule utilitarian might argue that there is greater utility when people are habituated to respect life, and suicide laws might be justified as a means of promoting that respect; and while Kant thinks that the religious argument against suicide casts the issue in its 'true light', he appears to offer a secular justification for such laws: suicide fails to treat humans as ends in themselves.

Rubin is aware of possible secular justifications for laws against assisted suicide. But he thinks that in our society at this time, suicide laws are based on "one particular specifically religious concept of morality and specifically reject rival concepts of morality" – unlike, say, laws against murder or slavery (794–5). "In our society, [it] seems clear that opposition to assisted suicide aligns with the Christian religion"; "proffered secular justifications are either too ill defined or insufficiently compelling" (797). There is some empirical evidence that he is correct: surveys of both the general public and physicians, in both the U.S. and elsewhere, indicate that those with no religious affiliation tend to be more supportive of euthanasia; in Western Europe between 1999 and 2008 support for euthanasia increased, and this was correlated with a strong decline in religiosity in Western Europe, whereas in post-communist Eastern Europe, where there was an increase in religiosity, there has been a decrease in acceptance of euthanasia and physician-assisted suicide; and a review of 15 surveys of UK physicians taken between 1990 and 2010 found the majority of physicians opposed legalizing euthanasia, with strength of religious views being the main correlative factor.[31] But even if Rubin is mistaken about what actually drives people to support laws against assisted suicide, and assuming that secular justifications of such laws convince some people – though I have argued that the rule-utilitarian defense is not convincing – these laws would still violate the principle of liberal pluralism.

30 See *Masterpiece Cakeshop v. Colorado Civil Rights Commission*, 138 S. Ct. 1719 (2017).

31 Emanuel et.al., "Attitudes and Practices," pp. 81, 83.

Encouraging, advising, assisting

While I have raised objections to suicide laws on the ground that punishing people because we think suicide is necessarily wrong is to impose one set of religious or philosophical beliefs on those who may not share those beliefs, there is a distinct reason we may want to punish people who *encourage* suicide or provide false information that leads someone to take their own life, even if we think that suicide itself is not necessarily wrong. In addressing this argument I return to distinctions I drew in chapter 3 between encouraging and inciting, advising, and assisting.

In chapter 3 I argued that Michelle did not 'assist' Conrad in killing himself – she did not help him rig the water pump that filled his truck with carbon monoxide, or do anything like load a rifle or supply heroin. In her texts she advised and encouraged him; when she told Conrad to 'get back in' his poison-filled truck, she encouraged him and may even have incited him to imminent action, though I would avoid using the word 'incited' if it falsely implies that she caused him to act.

Unlike assisting, advising and encouraging may violate an individual's autonomy. The principle of autonomy holds that so long as we don't harm others or prevent them from pursuing their legitimate self-regarding aims and, as Mill says, so long as we possess any tolerable amount of common sense and experience, we should be free to make our own decisions, not because our choice is most likely to be the best, but because it is our own choice. If someone makes a free and informed choice to kill themselves, and I assist them in achieving this goal, I help them realize their aims and *promote* their autonomy.[32] But unlike such assisting, advising and encouraging can sometimes undermine one's autonomy. When I *encourage* someone to kill themselves, I try to influence their will on a matter that above all others should be theirs to decide. If I use undue pressure, manipulation, or coercion, their decision may no longer be their own. When I just give *advice* to you about the best way to achieve your objective I do not necessarily try to influence your choice of objectives; but if I give misleading or false advice that you act on, I can undermine your autonomy by keeping you from achieving your desired goal.

The state has a legitimate interest in enacting regulations to ensure that I do not exercise my powers of persuasion in ways that violate your rights or your autonomy. If I encourage you to commit suicide, planting the idea in you and urging you on even though I know you don't want to die, I may

32 Using this principle, the state should not prohibit assisted suicide, but it should ensure the assistance is genuinely consented to – cf. Rubin, "Assisted Suicide, Morality, and Law," pp. 800–6.

act badly depending on my motives. But I don't necessarily violate any right you have. Interest groups, politicians, advertisers, op-ed writers, moral philosophers, and countless others all may encourage you to act against what you believe are your interests without undermining your autonomy. In the chapter 3 discussion of causation, I suggested two ways in which one's autonomy can be undermined. I might coerce you so that your action is not voluntary. The state should prohibit me from saying "if you don't kill yourself I will kill your family," as you have a right not to be coerced. But if I threaten to reveal a dark secret about your past and this causes you to kill yourself, it's not clear I have violated your rights. In chapter 3 I also discussed a gray area of cases in which I fan your predispositions or pull hard on your otherwise weak trigger, thereby causing you to act voluntarily. While you act voluntarily, I may have caused your voluntary act, and this may violate your autonomy. Recall *Stephenson v. State*: Stephenson kidnapped, assaulted, and raped Marge Oberholtzer, putting her in such a state of mind that she took poison, which caused her death. Stephenson did not coerce Ms. Oberholtzer to kill herself – he did not, for example, threaten to kill her loved ones unless she ingested poison. Rather, he caused her to want to take the poison, much like Sextus caused Lucretia to want to take her own life. On a theory of legal moralism, Stephenson could rightly be punished for putting his victim in a suicidal state of mind. But we needn't rely on a theory of legal moralism to punish him: we could punish him for kidnapping, assault, and rape. I leave open the question of whether there should be laws targeting those falling in the gray area of causing others to voluntarily commit a crime or cause harm. But laws that punish me for encouraging you to commit suicide when I do not coerce you or otherwise diminish your autonomy, on the ground that doing so goes against the moral sensibilities of the majority even though it violates no right, are grounded in a theory of legal moralism that is deeply problematic and counter to the principle of liberal pluralism. This is so even if my motives are malevolent.

Michelle did not violate Conrad's autonomy. She did not overbear his will. She was trying to persuade Conrad to do something that he had expressed a desire to do and had attempted in the past, something she apparently came to believe was in his own interest. Nor did she provide false or misleading information to Conrad that he relied on in killing himself. While we should reject laws that broadly prohibit encouraging or assisting suicide, a more narrowly tailored law might be justified if it prohibited coercion or bullying or maliciously providing false information to manipulate someone into acting against their true will. But Michelle would not have violated such a law.

6 Conclusion

I understand why many people wanted Michelle Carter to be punished: in the weeks before his death she encouraged Conrad Roy to kill himself and gave advice about the best methods, instead of seeking help for him. At the very moment when he was close to completing the deed, he hesitated, he sought her out, and she told him to 'get back in' a toxic truck, knowing that if he did he would almost surely die. Conrad seems to have heeded her words. But for those words, Conrad may not have died on or about July 13, 2014, in a K-Mart parking lot. He might have eventually received effective treatment that brought him out of his depression. While it is troubling to punish people for their speech, even some of the staunchest defenders of free speech do not think individuals should be able to incite others to cause harm.

Ms. Carter has been tried and convicted in the court of public opinion. ABC's *20/20* report included interviews with Conrad's relatives, who chastised Michelle for having the audacity to attend Conrad's wake. NBC titled its *Dateline* episode on the case "Reckless." Justice Cordy of the Massachusetts Supreme Judicial Court accused Ms. Carter of conducting a "systematic campaign of coercion" to end Conrad's life. A comment published in the *Harvard Law Review* compared what Michelle did to the actions of a man who kidnapped, assaulted, and raped a woman who then took poison to end her life. A recent movie about the Carter case, while not entirely one-sided, portrays Michelle as trying to get attention so that her friends would spend time with her. She is annoying and irksome and concerned only about herself, as if she encouraged Conrad to kill himself to get hugs and feel important.[1]

I have attempted to counterbalance the preceding reactions. News media, prosecutors, and judges have presented Ms. Carter as a villain, relying on snippets of conversations, the most damning of which we know of only by

1 Stephen Tonkin, *Conrad and Michelle: If Words Could Kill*, first broadcast on Lifetime (September 23, 2018).

Michelle's recollection months later. They seldom refer to the numerous texts in which she expressed love for Conrad, an attitude that would explain why she would want to attend the wake. They tend to ignore how Michelle, for months if not years, tried to dissuade Conrad from killing himself and encouraged him to seek help. They ignore how Michelle saw Conrad experience debilitating depression and could sincerely have come to believe he would be better off 'in heaven'. While quick to blame Michelle for not being more persistent in persuading Conrad to get help, they do not consider whether other people close to Conrad might also share in the responsibility for his death.

I have argued that the state prosecutors should have used their discretion and declined to charge Ms. Carter with a criminal offense. Michelle violated no law. Suicide is not illegal, nor, in Massachusetts, is assisting or encouraging suicide. The prosecutor resorted to a virtually unprecedented application of the law against involuntary manslaughter that required the state to show that Ms. Carter wantonly and recklessly caused Conrad's death. To make that case the state would have to prove a counterfactual and show that Conrad did not act voluntarily but was under Michelle's command.

While I've presented a case against punishing Ms. Carter, I have not denied that Ms. Carter acted badly and is morally blameworthy. While I do not think she caused harm, coerced Conrad, or violated anyone's rights, she did encourage Conrad to kill himself. Instead, I argued that we should be reluctant to morally punish her based on snippets that may leave out crucial information we need to fairly assess her character and conduct. I also argued that even if Michelle acted badly, we should not legally punish individuals because we don't think they are morally virtuous. I presented objections to laws against encouraging suicide by appealing to the theory of liberal pluralism. The view that suicide or its encouragement is wrong is most predominantly rooted in a religious conception that all human life – even a life of pain and suffering – is sacred and that it is a sin against God to end it before it runs its natural course; and in a liberal pluralist society the state should not impose a religious view on those who do not share it. Of course the state should prevent people from using coercion or bullying tactics to manipulate individuals into killing themselves, and provide resources for counseling, education, and other measures to preempt impulsive suicides.

While I presented the case against punishing Ms. Carter legally or morally, the point I am even more committed to advancing in this book is that whatever judgment we ultimately reach, it should be based not merely on our intuitions and gut instincts, but upon a consideration of the fundamental issues of moral, political, and legal theory the case raises. Whether Ms. Carter should have been sent to prison is an important question. But the case has much broader implications, for privacy, for our practice of punishment, for how we hold people accountable for their actions, for the scope of free speech, and for the toleration we afford to people with different religious and philosophical worldviews who must live together in a pluralist society. But not everyone appears to agree that theory matters.

Haidt's argument: reason vs. intuition

In chapter 1 I introduced the views of the social psychologist Jonathan Haidt, who takes the position that we intrinsically judge others by relying on instinct, emotion, intuition, and perception rather than on our higher cognitive functions including reason. Haidt has us think of ourselves as consisting of an elephant and a rider; the elephant has been around longer and guides us with emotions, intuition, and feelings such as disgust or loyalty. The rider, who emerged later with the development of higher brain functioning, does not steer the elephant, as rationalist philosophers think, but instead develops after the fact explanations for what the elephant does.[2] This is, on his view, why it can be so hard to reason with people (xx–xxi). People will formulate post-hoc rationalizations for their immediate judgments and even stick to them in the face of countervailing evidence (28–29).

Haidt seems resigned to this fact of human nature that we form judgments based on pre-deliberative intuitions. He refers to himself as an intuitionist and rejects what he calls the 'rationalist delusion' (103). At one point he blames two of the philosophers I have drawn on – Bentham and Kant – for taking 'moral science' on a 200-year tangent with their rationalism (135), and suggests that the hyper-rationalist Bentham lacked the empathy that drives most of us because he may have had Asperger's syndrome (140).

Haidt does say that elephants are sometimes open to reason (79). As evidence, he cites a study in which some Harvard students were asked their reaction to consensual incest. Some were first told a really bad argument to justify consensual incest – 'there would be more love in the world'; others were given a stronger supporting argument – that the aversion to incest is really caused by an evolutionary adaptation to avoid birth defects – and in the scenario they were asked to react to, contraception was used so that this concern would not be relevant. The subjects' reaction to incest was negative regardless of which argument they were given. But when some subjects were forced to wait 2 minutes and reflect on the good argument, they were more tolerant of incest.[3] Haidt concludes that the "quick a

2 Jonathan Haidt, *The Righteous Mind* (New York: Vintage Books, 2012), p. 54.

3 Haidt, *The Righteous Mind*, p. 81; referring to J.M. Paxton, L. Ungar, and J. Greene, "Reflection and Reasoning in Moral Judgment," *Cognitive Science*, 36(1):163–77 (2012).

ffective flashes" resulting from our elephant can be changed by the rider given sufficient time (45–6, 81). But, Haidt insists, this is "rare" (54).

Haidt sees psychology as descriptive: it explains how the moral mind actually works, not how it ought to work (141). He might explain the hostility many people have toward Ms. Carter as driven by a pre-reflective ethic of divinity or community (116–17) that regards Michelle's encouragement of suicide as sacrilegious and destructive of family and community bonds. He might say that those who support Ms. Carter are guided by a pre-reflective ethic that values autonomy and individual rights.

I have written this book under the assumption that moral judgments should be based on deliberation and analysis rather than gut feelings. The conclusions drawn by prosecutors, defense attorneys, judges, the news media, and much of the public about Ms. Carter's blameworthiness rest on inferences from carefully selected texts between Michelle and her friends that are subject to interpretation. We should avoid interpreting the facts selectively according to our instinctual biases – we need to resist the forces that Haidt points to as the determinants of our moral judgments. Haidt admits that we can resist these forces. He thinks it is hard to do so, but we should make the effort. Being driven by our elephant may be part of our nature, but as we know from the development of gene therapies, corrective lenses for failing eyesight, surgically implanted prosthetic devices and artificial organs, and countless other examples, we can overcome our defective natures.

Privacy

There is another underlying theme that I want to return to in concluding. I have emphasized the importance of privacy in providing a space to express ourselves without being morally judged and publicly shamed. But I also recognized that privacy should not unduly shield harmful conduct from public exposure. I have argued that while the police acted lawfully in acquiring the texts between Michelle and Conrad because they had secured a search warrant, the prosecutor should not have made these texts publicly available by prosecuting Michelle. The privacy interest that Michelle could claim in her texts outweighs the public's interest in legally or morally punishing her. I reached this conclusion only after considering factors such as whether she was the morally and legally relevant cause of Conrad's death, which hinges on whether she coerced Conrad. But we could work through these issues only by having access to her texts. For example, in chapter 3 I used texts that showed Conrad rebuffing Michelle's numerous attempts to get closer to him to conclude that she did not have the power over Conrad that would have enabled her to coerce him. Given that I concede that privacy is a value that must be weighed against competing values such as the control of crime, we are faced with a puzzle. How can we object to acquiring access to the texts between Michelle and Conrad if we need those texts to determine whether she caused harm or committed a crime, questions we must resolve in order to determine whether privacy interests outweigh the state's competing interests?

This dilemma could be resolved if courts could have access to private records they could review behind closed doors without making them available to the public. This currently is not the practice in the United States, where even the name of a rape victim, if appearing in a court document, is fair game for journalists to publish.[4] In some countries, however, court dockets do not include the name of the accused, which remains private.[5] The decision of what information is newsworthy involves a balancing of interests, and while in the United States courts give much greater weight to free speech, this result is not inevitable.[6]

Another way to prevent undue invasions of privacy besides redacting court records would be for prosecutors to factor into their decision of whether to press charges and make the texts a matter of public record the uncertainty of establishing a clear and convincing judgment about a morally nebulous issue as to causation and to weigh in their calculation the consequences for privacy and free speech of punishing someone on the basis of what they reveal in their texts. Having now looked at all of Michelle's texts that were introduced into the public record, rather than incendiary snippets, we have reason to doubt her ability to coerce Conrad. One might now even question whether the police had probable cause to suspect that Michelle committed a crime consisting of her coercing Conrad and causing his death, especially given his predisposition to suicide, which the police presumably were aware of after interviewing Conrad's loved ones and investigating his prior history. To the extent that judges and law enforcers were guided in their assessment by pre-reflective influences that slanted their weighing of the evidence against Michelle, it is to that degree important to be aware of Haidt's argument about the instinctual forces that shape our judgments, and to resist these forces.

4 *Florida Star v. BJF*, 491 U.S. 524 (1989).

5 James Jacobs and Elena Larrauri, "Are Criminal Convictions a Public Matter? The USA and Spain," *Punishment and Society* 14(2):3–28 (2012).

6 See Mark Tunick, *Balancing Privacy and Free Speech: Unwanted Attention in the Age of Social Media* (London: Routledge, 2015).

Index

accountability *see* punishment
advice: as not the most proximate cause 54–5; as protected speech 54–5; justified restrictions on 54; vs. advisory inducement 54n24; vs. assisting 48–9, 67–8; vs. encouragement 48, 55–61, 67–8, 92, 105–6; vs. incitement 55, 60–1
Arendt, Hannah 46n10
assisting *see* advice
Augustine, Saint 94
Austin, J.L. 46n19
autonomy 68, 91, 101, 106; Conrad's, respected by Michelle 63; undermining of by false information 68, 105–6; undermining of by undue influence 63, 91–2, 105–6; *see also* coercion

Bentham, Jeremy: Haidt's criticism of 109; on punishment 84–5; on suicide 92–3, 98; utilitarian theory of 84, 92
Berns, Walter *see* legal moralism; retributive theory
Billy Budd 37–8
Blackmun, Justice 79–80
Boardman, Samantha 10, 13–14, 20, 39
Bowers v. Hardwick 79–80
Brandenburg v. Ohio 60n31
Breggin, Dr. Peter 75
Burger, Chief Justice Warren 102
but for cause *see* causation

Cannibal Cop 26–7
Carpenter v. U.S. 34–5
Carter, Michelle: accountability of 75; attempts to help Conrad of 1, 5–9, 44–5, 63, 108; deterrability of 85–6, 87, 88n27; eating disorder of 5, 6; expectations of privacy of 19, 33–4; frustration of with Conrad's depression 1, 7–8, 90; as inciter of Conrad? 61, 105; mental health of 15; moral blameworthiness of 41, 43–4, 108; public reaction to 2, 3, 38, 107; relationship of with Conrad 5, 60, 62, 63–7, 110; texts of 4, 5–14, 19, 50–2, 56–8, 63–6, 90; texts of that encourage or may pressure Conrad 9, 11–12, 56–8, 63–6; trial and sentence of viii, 15–16, 44, 45
Cataldo, Joseph (defense attorney) 15
causation: but for 45–6, 68; complexity of the concept of 45; proximate 15, 29, 46–54, 61, 68; legal vs. scientific 45–6, 53–4; of voluntary acts 55, 58–9, 61, 106; *see also* Feinberg, Joel, on causation; voluntary intervention principle
Chaplinksy v. New Hampshire 49n18
Christianity, and suicide 103, 104
City of Ontario v. Quon 34
Clementi, Tyler 26n11
coercion: of Conrad by Michelle? 40–1, 62–67, 81, 106, 110; hypnosis as 59, 63; threats as 63; and the voluntary intervention principle 62
Cohen-Almagor, Raphael 61n32
common law offense 41

Commonwealth v. Carter 42n1, 60n30, 62n34, 90n2
Commonwealth v. Catalina 47, 48
Commonwealth v. Kean 21n2
Commonwealth v. Rosado 46n11
comprehensive doctrines 83–4, 100, 101
Conly, Sarah 82, 84, 93–4, 100–1
Conrad and Michelle: If Words Could Kill (film) 107
Conradt, Louis 26n11
CO poisoning 1, 14–15, 40, 43, 44, 46, 62; google searches on 11, 53; Michelle's advice about 50, 51–2; website on 51, 52
Cordy, Justice 47, 60, 62, 66, 90, 107
Cruzan v. Director, Missouri Department of Health 99

Dateline NBC *see* media coverage of Carter case
deterrence 69, 72, 85, 87–8; ineffectiveness of if law is unclear 41, 60, 87–8; Kantian objection to 88; *see also* punishment
Doe v. Luster 70
duty: to intervene 42–3; legal vs. moral 43–44; vs. obligation 42

encouraging *see* advice; suicide, wrongness of encouraging
euthanasia 67–8, 90; attitudes toward 104
Experiment in Terror 63

Feinberg, Joel 22n6, 54n25, 74n8, 81n17; offense to others principle of 78, 82; on causation 53–4, 58–9; on causing voluntary acts 58–9, 61
Fetsch v. City of Roseburg 31, 33
First Amendment Establishment Clause 102; and suicide laws 100, 102–104
First Amendment Free Speech clause 2–3, 44, 49–50, 52–54; and slippery slope argument 53, 54; and speech integral to criminal conduct 2–3, 49–50, 55–6, 61; *see also* advice; Mill, J. S.; speech
Fourth Amendment 20–1; and private searches 21; state action requirement of 21
freedom of speech *see* First Amendment; speech
Fried, Charles 23

Giboney v. Empire Storage and Ice Co. 2–3, 49n18
Google 11, 46, 53

Haidt, Jonathan 3–4, 109–10
harm principle 81, 83–4; *see also* Mill, harm principle of; suicide, and harm principle
Hegel, G.W.F. *see* retributive theory
Hill, Anita 24
Hit Man 52–3
Hoffa v. U.S. 30n17, 32, 33, 35
Holmes, Justice Oliver Wendell 55, 79–80
Hume, David, on suicide 97–8

incitement 55, 61, 105; *see also* advice, vs. incitement
interests: vs. desires 22; in newsworthy information 69, 70–1
intuition, vs. reason vii–viii, 3–4, 109–10
involuntary manslaughter 21–2; as charge for assisting in suicide 22, 41, 87–8, 108; by commission 17, 42, 44–67; by omission 17, 42–44; vs. homicide 41–2

Jessica Jones 63

Kant, Immanuel: liberal theory of 73, 100; on suicide 78, 97, 98, 104; *see also* retributive theory
Katz v. United States 28–9, 30, 33, 37
Kilgrave 63, 67
Kipnis, Kenneth 86n25

Larrauri, Elena 111n5
legal moralism: Berns's defense of 78; criticism of 79–84, 91; as rejection of the harm principle 81, 83; as a theory of what should be illegal 76,

77–8, 83; as a theory of why we punish 77–9
Lemon Test 102
Lemon v. Kurtzman 102n27
liberalism 80–82, 83–4, 91–2, 105–6; *see also* legal moralism, criticism of; liberal pluralism
liberal pluralism 83–4, 99–102, 104
Livy 94
Locke, John on suicide 97
Loewy, Arnold 28
Lucretia, Rape of 94, 106
Lynch v. Donnelly 102n28

Mabbott, J.D. *see* retributive theory
Masterpiece Cakeshop v. Colorado Civil Rights Commission 104
McLean, G.R. 98n17
media coverage of Carter case 4, 9, 13–14, 38, 62, 107–8
Melville, Herman 37–8
Mill, J.S.: on capital punishment 93, 95; corn dealer example of 55–6, 60–1; defense of liberty of 23, 55–6, 80; harm principle of 61, 78, 80–2, 100; on suicide 93, 98
Moniz, Judge 16, 62, 66
Monteith, Cory 50

obligations: vs. duty 42 *see also* prima facie obligations
O'Conner, Justice Sandra Day 102
oyako shinju 101–2

paternalism 77; coercive 82–3, 84, 93–4, 100
People v. Duffy 47–8
People v. Oliver 43
performatives 49
Persampieri v. Commonwealth 48, 58
Philosophers Brief on the right to die 99–100
plain view principle 20–1, 23, 28, 36
prima facie obligations 20
private searches *see* Fourth Amendment
privacy: balancing of against other interests 16–17, 25, 27, 35–9, 69; and the Carter case 68–9, 110–11; and friendship 23–4, 27; and punishment 25–7, 110; in public records 71, 111; snippet theory of 24–5, 37, 68–9, 108; and third party doctrine 30–35; value of 16, 20, 23–27, 37; *see also* reasonable expectations of privacy
proximate cause *see* causation
punishment: and accountability 75; moral (or non-legal) vs. legal 1–2, 25–7, 37–9, 41, 71, 75–6, 108; private 26–7, 38; retributive theory of 71–2, 73–9; utilitarian theory of 72, 84–8; *see also* legal moralism

Rawls, John: on political liberalism 83–4, 100; on rule utilitarianism 86n26, 95–6
Rayburn, Katie (prosecutor) 15
reasonable expectations of privacy 20–1, 22–3, 27; of the dead 34; Katz test of 28–9; in relations of trust 31–2, 33–4; in smart phones 34; in texts 29–35; and totality of circumstances test 36; *see also* plain view principle
reckless conduct 44–5
retributive theory: of Berns 77–9; of Hegel 74–5, 78–9, 88; of Kant 73–4, 78–9, 88; of Mabbott 76–7, 78–9; vs. revenge 72; *see also* legal moralism; punishment
reverse psychology 10–11, 14
Rice v. The Paladin Enterprises 52–3, 60
rights: to not be coerced 81; to die 99–100; not violated by assisting or encouraging suicide 60–1, 81–2, 104; violation of as criterion for harm 61, 78–9, 81
Riley v. California 34
Romeo and Juliet 7, 65, 93–4
Rosen, Jeffrey 24–5, 37
Roy, Conrad: circumstances of death of 1, 13–16, 40, 46, 66–7, 90; expectations of privacy of 19, 33–4; mental health of 6, 8; predisposition to suicide of 5–6, 8, 40, 45, 59, 61, 90; relationship of with parents 12, 38–9, 85
Rubin, Edward 103–4,105n32

rule utilitarianism: criticism of 95–6; as defense of suicide laws 86, 94–5, 104; defined 86, 94

Schenck v. U.S. 55n26
Smith v. Maryland 32–3, 35
speech: chilling of if we punish advice or encouragement 53–4, 60, 87, 88–9; public vs. private 60–1; symbolic 45; vs. conduct 44–5, 48–50, 67–8; *see also* First Amendment; performatives
State v. Bone 32
State v. Carle 31, 33
State v. Clampitt 32
State v. Duchow 35–6
State v. Goucher 31, 33
State v. Hinton 33–4, 35
State v. Martinez 21n2
State v. Melchert-Dinkel 49n17, 68n36
State v. Patino 31–2, 33
State v. Tentoni 30–1, 34, 45, 52
Stephenson v. State 48, 53, 59, 62, 94n10, 106
suicide: and the harm principle 60–1, 81–2; legality of 21, 41, 71, 99; legality of assisting in 18, 68, 75, 91, 99; and liberal pluralism 83–4, 99–102, 104, 108; of Lucretia 94, 106; by teenagers who may make cognitive errors 93; theistic objection to 83, 91, 97–9, 100; wrongness of encouraging 91, 97, 105–6, 108; *see also* euthanasia; Hume, David, on suicide; Kant, Immanuel, on suicide; Locke, John, on suicide; utilitarianism, and suicide laws
synechdode argument 24–5, 37

Ten, C.L. 95n12
Texas v. Johnson 44n7
texting: as conversation 29, 47; as proximate cause 47; vs. face to face interaction 29, 30, 47, 63; vs. letters 29, 47; vs. phone conversations 29, 30, 33, 47; *see also* reasonable expectations of privacy
third party doctrine *see* privacy
Thomas, Clarence 24–5
toleration 24, 83–4
Tunick, Mark 22n6, 25–7, 28n14, 72, 73n7, 84n24, 96n13, 102n26, 111n6

U.S. v. O'Brien 44n6
utilitarianism 72, 84, 92; and rejection of higher law 92, 94–5; and suicide laws 85–8, 92–6; *see also* deterrence; punishment; rule utilitarianism

Volokh, Eugene 3n1, 49n18
voluntary intervention principle 48, 54–5, 59–61, 106

Waldron, Jeremy 80n15, 100
Walzer, Michael 24, 35
warrant: in Carter case 21, 22, 30; Fourth Amendment requirement to have 21, 22, 34
Webstad v. Stortini 42–3, 62

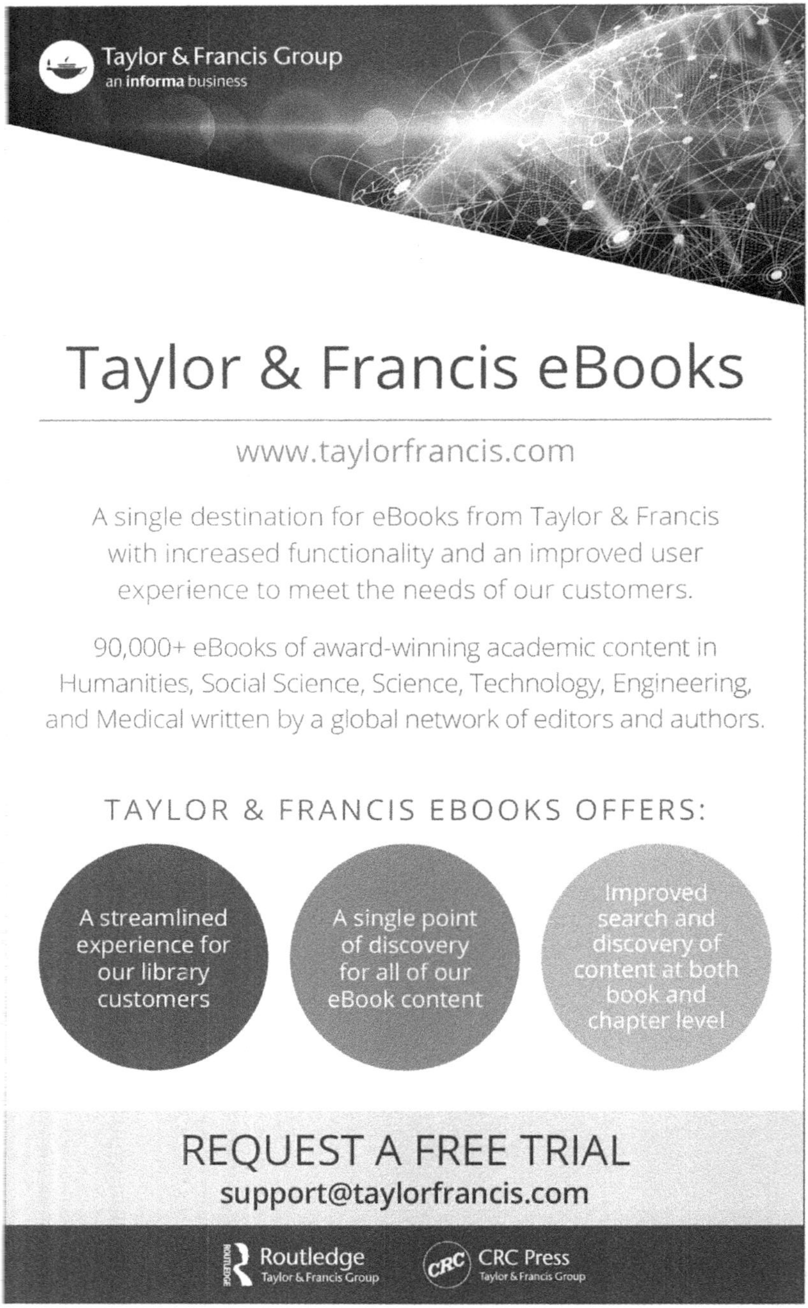
Taylor & Francis Group
an informa business
Taylor & Francis eBooks
www.taylorfrancis.com
A single destination for eBooks from Taylor & Francis with increased functionality and an improved user experience to meet the needs of our customers.
90,000+ eBooks of award-winning academic content in Humanities, Social Science, Science, Technology, Engineering, and Medical written by a global network of editors and authors.
TAYLOR & FRANCIS EBOOKS OFFERS:
A streamlined experience for our library customers
A single point of discovery for all of our eBook content
Improved search and discovery of content at both book and chapter level
REQUEST A FREE TRIAL
support@taylorfrancis.com
Routledge
Taylor & Francis Group
CRC Press
Taylor & Francis Group